UNLOCKING
THE BIBLE

NEW TESTAMENT BOOK I

The Hinge of History

UNLOCKING THE BIBLE

NEW TESTAMENT BOOK I

The Hinge of History

David Pawson

with Andy Peck

Marshall Pickering
An Imprint of HarperCollins*Publishers*

Marshall Pickering is an imprint of
HarperCollins*Religious*
Part of HarperCollins*Publishers*
77–85 Fulham Palace Road, London W6 8JB

First published in Great Britain in 1999
by HarperCollins*Religious*

1 3 5 7 9 10 8 6 4 2

A catalogue record for this book is
available from the British Library

ISBN 0 551 03187 5

Printed and bound in Great Britain by
Caledonian International Book Manufacturing Ltd, Glasgow

CONTENTS

INTRODUCTION

I suppose this all started in Arabia, in 1957. I was then a chaplain in the Royal Air Force, looking after the spiritual welfare of all those who were not C.E. (Church of England) or R.C. (Roman Catholic) but O.D. (other denominations – Methodist to Salvationist, Buddhist to atheist). I was responsible for a string of stations from the Red Sea to the Persian Gulf. In most there was not even a congregation to call a 'church', never mind a building.

In civilian life I had been a Methodist minister working anywhere from the Shetland Islands to the Thames Valley. In that denomination it was only necessary to prepare a few sermons each quarter, which were hawked around a 'circuit' of chapels. Mine had mostly been of the 'text' type (talking about a single verse) or the 'topic' type (talking about a single subject with many verses from all over the Bible). In both I was as guilty as any of taking texts out of context before I realized that chapter and verse numbers were neither inspired nor intended by God and had done immense damage to Scripture, not least by changing the meaning of 'text' from a whole book to a single sentence. The Bible had become a compendium of 'proof-texts', picked out at will and used to support almost anything a preacher wanted to say.

With a pocketful of sermons based on this questionable technique, I found myself in uniform, facing very different congregations – all male instead of the lifeboat-style gatherings I had been used to: women and children first. My meagre stock of messages soon ran out. Some of them had gone down like a lead balloon, especially in compulsory parade services in England before I was posted overseas.

So here I was in Aden, virtually starting a church from scratch, from the Permanent Staff and temporary National Servicemen of Her Majesty's youngest armed service. How could I get these men interested in the Christian faith and then committed to it?

Something (I would now say: Someone) prompted me to announce that I would give a series of talks over a few months, which would take us right through the Bible ('from Generation to Revolution'!).

It was to prove a voyage of discovery for all of us. The Bible became a new book when seen as a whole. To use a well-worn cliché, we had failed to see the wood for the trees. Now God's plan and purpose were unfolding in a fresh way. The men were getting something big enough to sink their teeth into. The thought of being part of a cosmic rescue was a powerful motivation. The Bible story was seen as both real and relevant.

Of course, my 'overview' was at that time quite simple, even naive. I felt like that American tourist who 'did' the British Museum in 20 minutes – and could have done it in 10 if he'd had his running shoes! We raced through the centuries, giving some books of the Bible little more than a passing glance.

But the results surpassed my expectations and set the course for the rest of my life and ministry. I had become a 'Bible teacher', albeit in embryo. My ambition to share the excitement of knowing the whole Bible became a passion.

When I returned to 'normal' church life, I resolved to take my congregation through the whole Bible in a decade (if they put up with me that long). This involved tackling about one 'chapter' at every service. This took a lot of time, both in preparation (an hour in the study for every 10 minutes in the pulpit) and delivery (45–50 minutes). The ratio was similar to that of cooking and eating a meal.

The effect of this systematic 'exposition' of Scripture confirmed its rightness. A real hunger for God's Word was revealed. People began to *come* from far and wide, 'to recharge their batteries' as some explained. Soon this traffic was reversed. Tape recordings, first prepared for the sick and housebound, now began to *go* far and wide, ultimately in hundreds of thousands to 120 countries. No one was more surprised than I.

Leaving Gold Hill in Buckinghamshire for Guildford in Surrey, I found myself sharing in the design and building of the Millmead Centre, which contained an ideal auditorium for continuing this teaching ministry. When it was opened, we decided to associate it with the whole Bible by reading it aloud right through without stopping. It took us 84 hours, from Sunday evening until Thursday morning, each person reading for 15 minutes before passing the Bible on to someone else. We used the 'Living' version, the easiest both to read and to listen to, with the heart as well as the mind.

We did not know what to expect, but the event seemed to capture the public imagination. Even the mayor wanted to take part and by sheer coincidence (or providence) found himself reading about a husband who was 'well known, for he sits in the council chamber with the other civic leaders'. He insisted on taking a copy home for his wife. Another lady dropped in on her way to see her solicitor about the legal termination of her marriage and found herself reading, 'I hate divorce, says the Lord'. She never went to the lawyer.

An aggregate of 2,000 people attended and bought half a ton of Bibles. Some came for half an hour and were still there hours later, muttering to themselves, 'Well, maybe just one more book and then I really must go.'

It was the first time many, including our most regular attenders, had ever heard a book of the Bible read straight through. In most churches only a few sentences are read each week and then not always consecutively. What other book would get anyone interested, much less excited, if treated in this way?

So on Sundays we worked through the whole Bible book by book. For the Bible is not one book, but many – in fact, it is a whole library (the word *biblia* in Latin and Greek is plural: 'books'). And not just many books, but many *kinds* of books – history, law, letters, songs, etc. It became necessary, when we had finished studying one book, and were starting on another, to begin with a special introduction covering very basic questions: What kind of book is this? When was it written? Who wrote it? Who was it written for? Above all, *why* was it written? The answer to that one provided the 'key' to unlock its message. Nothing in that book could be fully understood unless seen as part of the whole. The context of every 'text' was not just the paragraph or the section but fundamentally the whole book itself.

By now, I was becoming more widely known as a Bible teacher and was invited to colleges, conferences and conventions – at first in this country, but increasingly overseas, where tapes had opened doors and prepared the way. I enjoy meeting new people and seeing new places, but the novelty of sitting in a jumbo jet wears off in 10 minutes!

Everywhere I went I found the same eager desire to know God's Word. I praised God for the invention of recording cassettes which, unlike video systems, are standardized the world over. They were helping to plug a real hole in so many places.

There is so much successful evangelism but so little teaching ministry to stabilize, develop and mature converts.

I might have continued along these lines until the end of my active ministry, but the Lord had another surprise for me, which was the last link in the chain that led to the publication of these volumes.

In the early 1990s, Bernard Thompson, a friend pastoring a church in Wallingford, near Oxford, asked me to speak at a short series of united meetings with the aim of increasing interest in and knowledge of the Bible – an objective guaranteed to hook me!

I said I would come once a month and speak for three hours about one book in the Bible (with a coffee break in the middle!). In return, I asked those attending to read that book right through before and after my visit. During the following weeks preachers were to base their sermons and house groups their discussions on the same book. All this would hopefully mean familiarity at least with that one book.

My purpose was two-fold. On the one hand, to get people so interested in that book that they could hardly wait to read it. On the other hand, to give them enough insight and information so that when they did read it they would be excited by their ability to understand it. To help with both, I used pictures, charts, maps and models.

This approach really caught on. After just four months I was pressed to book dates for the next five years, to cover all 66 books! I laughingly declined, saying I might be in heaven long before then (in fact, I have rarely booked anything more than six months ahead, not wanting to mortgage the future, or presume that I have one). But the Lord had other plans and enabled me to complete the marathon.

Anchor Recordings (72, The Street, Kennington, Ashford, Kent TN24 9HS) have distributed my tapes for the last 20 years and when the Director, Jim Harris, heard the recordings of these meetings, he urged me to consider putting them on video. He arranged cameras and crew to come to High Leigh Conference Centre, its main hall 'converted' into a studio, for three days at a time, enabling 18 programmes to be made with an invited audience. It took another five years to complete this project, which was distributed under the title 'Unlocking the Bible'.

Now these videos are travelling around the world. They are being used in house groups, churches, colleges, the armed forces, gypsy camps, prisons and on cable television networks. During an extended visit to Malaysia, they were being snapped up at a rate of a thousand a week. They have infiltrated all six continents, including Antarctica!

More than one have called this my 'legacy to the church'. Certainly it is the fruit of many years' work. And I am now in my seventieth year on planet earth, though I do not think the Lord has finished with me yet. But I did think this particular task had reached its conclusion. I was mistaken.

HarperCollins approached me with a view to publishing this material in a series of volumes. For the last decade or so I had been writing books for other publishers, so was already convinced that this was a good means of spreading God's Word. Nevertheless, I had two huge reservations about this proposal which made me very hesitant. One was due to the way the material had been prepared and the other related to the way it had been delivered. I shall explain them in reverse order.

First, I have never written out in full any sermon, lecture or talk. I speak from notes, sometimes pages of them. I have been concerned about communication as much as content and intuitively knew that a full manuscript interrupts the rapport between speaker and audience, not least by diverting his eyes from the listeners. Speech that is more spontaneous can respond to reactions as well as express more emotions.

The result is that my speaking and writing styles are very different, each adapted to its own function. I enjoy listening to my tapes and can be deeply moved by myself. I am enthusiastic about reading one of my new publications, often telling my wife, 'This really *is* good stuff!' But when I read a transcript of what I have said, I am ashamed and even appalled. Such repetition of words and phrases! Such rambling, even incomplete sentences! Such a mixture of verb tenses, particularly past and present! Do I really abuse the Queen's English like this? The evidence is irrefutable.

I made it clear that I could not possibly contemplate writing out all this material in full. It has taken most of one lifetime anyway and I do not have another. True, transcripts of the talks had already been made, with a view to translating and dubbing the videos into other languages such as Spanish and Chinese. But the thought of these being printed as they were horrified me. Perhaps this is a final struggle with pride, but the contrast with my written books, over which I took such time and trouble, was more than I could bear.

I was assured that copy editors correct most grammatical blunders. But the main remedy proposed was to employ a 'ghostwriter' who was in tune with me and my ministry, to adapt the material for printing. An introduction to the person chosen, Andy Peck, gave me every confidence that he could do the job, even though the result would not be what I would have written – nor, for that matter, what he would have written himself.

I gave him all the notes, tapes, videos and transcripts, but these volumes are as much his work as mine. He has worked incredibly hard and I am deeply grateful to him for enabling me to reach many more with the truth that sets people free. If one gets a prophet's reward for merely giving the prophet a drink of water, I can only thank the Lord for the reward Andy will get for this immense labour of love.

Second, I have never kept careful records of my sources. This is partly because the Lord blessed me with a reasonably good memory for such things as quotations and illustrations and perhaps also because I have never used secretarial assistance.

Books have played a major role in my work – three tons of them, according to the last furniture remover we employed, filling two rooms and a garden shed. They are in three categories: those I have read, those I intend to read and those I will never read! They have been such a blessing to me and such a bane to my wife.

The largest section by far is filled with Bible commentaries. When preparing a Bible study, I have looked up all relevant writers, but only after I have prepared as much as I can on my own. Then I have both added to and corrected my efforts in the light of scholarly and devotional writings.

It would be impossible to name all those to whom I have been indebted. Like many others, I devoured William Barclay's *Daily Bible Readings* as soon as they were issued back in the 1950s. His knowledge of New Testament background and vocabulary was invaluable and his simple and clear style a model to follow, though I later came to question his 'liberal' interpretations. John Stott, Merill Tenney, Gordon Fee and William Hendrickson were among those who opened up the New Testament for me, while Alec Motyer, G. T. Wenham and Derek Kidner did the same for the Old. And time would fail to tell of Denney, Lightfoot, Nygren, Robinson, Adam Smith, Howard, Ellison, Mullen, Ladd, Atkinson, Green, Beasley-Murray, Snaith, Marshall, Morris, Pink and many many others. Nor must I forget two remarkable little books from the pens of women: *What the Bible is all about* by Henrietta Mears and *Christ in all the Scriptures* by A. M. Hodgkin. To have sat at their feet has been an inestimable privilege. I have always

regarded a willingness to learn as one of the fundamental qual-
ifications to be a teacher.

I soaked up all these sources like a sponge. I remembered so
much of *what* I read, but could not easily recall *where* I had read
it. This did not seem to matter too much when gathering material for preaching, since most of these writers were precisely
aiming to help preachers and did not expect to be constantly
quoted. Indeed, a sermon full of attributed quotations can be
distracting, if not misinterpreted as name-dropping or indirectly
claiming to be well read. As could my previous paragraph!

But printing, unlike preaching, is subject to copyright,
since royalties are involved. And the fear of breaching this held
me back from allowing any of my spoken ministry to be repro-
duced in print. It would be out of the question to trace back 40
years' scrounging and even if that were possible, the necessary
footnotes and acknowledgements could double the size and
price of these volumes.

The alternative was to deny access to this material for
those who could most benefit from it, which my publisher
persuaded me would be wrong. At least I was responsible for
collecting and collating it all, but I dare to believe that there is
sufficient original contribution to justify its release.

I can only offer an apology and my gratitude to all those
whose studies I have plundered over the years, whether in small
or large amounts, hoping they might see this as an example of
that imitation which is the sincerest form of flattery. To use
another quotation I read somewhere: 'Certain authors, speaking of their works, say "my book" ... They would do better to
say "our book" ... because there is in them usually more of other
people's than their own' (the original came from Pascal).

So here is 'our' book! I suppose I am what the French
bluntly call a 'vulgarizer'. That is someone who takes what the
academics teach and make it simple enough for the 'common'

people to understand. I am content with that. As one old lady said to me, after I had expounded a quite profound passage of Scripture, 'You broke it up small enough for us to take it in.' I have, in fact, always aimed to so teach that a 12-year-old boy could understand and remember my message.

Some readers will be disappointed, even frustrated, with the paucity of text references, especially if they want to check me out! But their absence is intentional. God gave us his Word in books, but not in chapters and verses. That was the work of two bishops, French and Irish, centuries later. It became easier to find a 'text' and to ignore context. How many Christians who quote John 3:16 can recite verses 15 and 16? Many no longer 'search the scriptures'; they simply look them up (given the numbers). So I have followed the apostles' habit of naming the authors only – 'as Isaiah or David or Samuel said'. For example, the Bible says that God whistles. Where on earth does it say that? In the book of Isaiah. Whereabouts? Go and find out for yourself. Then you'll also find out when he did and why he did. And you'll have the satisfaction of having discovered all that by yourself.

One final word. Behind my hope that these introductions to the Bible books will help you to get to know and love them more than you did lies a much greater and deeper longing – that you will also come to know better and love more the subject of all the books, the Lord himself. I was deeply touched by the remark of someone who had watched all the videos within a matter of days: 'I know so much more about the Bible now, but the biggest thing was that I felt the heart of God as never before.'

What more could a Bible teacher ask? May you experience the same as you read these pages and join me in saying: Praise Father, Son and Holy Spirit.

J. David Pawson
Sherborne St John, 1999

Yes I thought I knew my Bible
Reading piecemeal, hit or miss
Now a part of John or Matthew
Then a bit of Genesis

Certain chapters of Isaiah
Certain psalms, the twenty-third.
First of Proverbs, twelfth of Romans
Yes, I thought I knew the Word

But I found that thorough reading
Was a different thing to do
And the way was unfamiliar
When I read my Bible through.

You who like to play at Bible
Dip and dabble here and there
Just before you kneel all weary
Yawning through a hurried prayer.

You who treat this crown of writings
As you treat no other book
Just a paragraph disjointed
Just a crude impatient look.

Try a worthier procedure
Try a broad and steady view;
You will kneel in awesome wonder
When you read the Bible through.

Author unknown

THE GOSPELS

Introduction

The Bible is a library of books written by 40 different authors over 1,400 years. God did not choose to give us a compendium of texts with chapter and verse numbers, nor did he provide books of doctrine arranged systematically. Instead he gave us a library of **different types of literature**, as diverse as poetry and history, letters and revelation, in three different languages – mainly Greek and Hebrew, with a little Aramaic.

Variety

This library reflects the **unique personalities and perspectives** of the various authors, just as any two books in a public library would be unique according to the personalities of the writers. It is important to remember that the Holy Spirit, the divine 'editor' of the Bible, did not treat the authors as word processors, communicating his truth but bypassing their minds and hearts. He was the ultimate author, yet at the same time the individuals themselves were free to communicate in their own way. Indeed, few of the authors knew that what they wrote would one day be declared part of Holy Scripture.

With this in mind, apparent contradictions within the Bible can be often settled by examining the **authors' intentions**.

Take, for example, the controversy concerning Paul's assertion that we are saved by faith and not works, and James' teaching in his Epistle on the need for works. When Paul dealt with the subject of faith in Romans he anticipated a different set of questions and concerns than James. Paul is concerned that we do not seek to be saved by our works, James that works accompany faith and thus show it to be genuine.

Unity

In spite of this variety, the Bible demonstrates at the same time its divine authorship. There is one overall theme: the **unfolding drama of redemption**, which runs from Genesis to Revelation. Genesis 1–3 and Revelation 21–22 have remarkable similarities, despite being written 1,400 years apart, wonderfully reflecting God's hand. It is possible to recognize the unity of the Bible without assuming that this must also mean uniformity. Just as God is one but three persons, so his Word reflects both unity and diversity.

Approaches to Bible study

We need to bear these aspects in mind whenever we come to study the Bible. Two approaches are equally important:

1. Variety: analysing a book and seeing its **differences** from other books.
2. Unity: noting its **similarities** with other books, and how it fits into the whole.

Those with a liberal view of the Bible tend to focus on the variety, denying claims to unity. Those with an evangelical view focus on the unity, fearful that to focus on variety may reveal contradictions.

It is necessary to retain a balance between acknowledging the divine authorship and inherent unity of the Bible, and at the same time looking at each book as the work of a human being writing for a particular purpose. If we just focus on the divine authorship, we may unwittingly gain a wrong perspective on a vital area of truth, failing to notice the way in which different authors have treated a theme. We mistakenly treat the texts on any theme as if there is just one book with one message and one style, forgetting that God has used the unique situation of book and author to communicate his truth. On the other hand, if we just focus on the individuality of the book, we may forget that it is part of a library which God has put together, exhibiting a wonderful unity of theme and purpose.

The value of this approach is especially clear when we come to study the **Gospels**. At one level, there is a unity of theme as each writes of the good news of Jesus. They have the same time period, people and places on which to report, but each has a **particular focus and audience** in mind. This is especially the case with John's Gospel, as it stands apart so distinctly from the other three 'synoptics', which hold so much in common. As we look specifically at these differences, John's particular flavour will become apparent.

The Gospels

The Gospels are the nearest thing we have to a biography of Jesus, covering his life, death and resurrection. What few realize, however, is that they are written in a unique style, one which was previously unheard of in the first century and which has no modern literary counterpart. Careful readers will know that to interpret the Gospels properly they will need to see each verse in its immediate context *and* in the context of the book as a whole. This creates problems if they do not understand the *style* of literature they are reading. We need to clarify what kind of a book a 'Gospel' is before looking at them in individual detail.

What is a Gospel?

A Gospel is certainly not an autobiography, since Jesus never wrote any books, but it is not a straight biography either, because over one-third of the pages of each Gospel describe the death of Jesus. No biography would spend a third of its pages on its subject's death, however spectacular or tragic that death may be. Perhaps the best comparison with modern life is not from the literary world at all, but from the world of the media. A Gospel is like a **news bulletin**.

The English word 'gospel' is an Anglo-Saxon version of the Greek word *evangelion*, which was used in New Testament times to describe the announcement of shattering news by an emissary sent around the towns and villages of an area. The defeat of an enemy or the death of an emperor would be typical examples. In the same way a Gospel is a news announcement which conveys straight away that this is exciting news to share. The implication is that the world will never be the same again once this news is heard.

Just as news is generally read aloud to hearers, so the Gospels were intended to be read aloud (in common with the rest of the New Testament). We can derive much benefit today if we too read them aloud (even just to ourselves) as well as silently.

Why were they written?

The reason for the Gospels being written in the form we have them is clear. In the early decades following Christ's ascension the Church grew in numbers and spread across the Roman world as the apostles spread the gospel message. Thus many people wanted the 'news' from those who had seen the events of Jesus' life first-hand. It became imperative that the **witnesses** to what Jesus did and said wrote down **reliable accounts** of his life and times.

Why are there four?

The first thing that strikes many people is that there are four Gospels which overlap considerably in content and wording. To some people it seems superfluous that there should be four, especially if they are saying the same thing, as they appear to do. Would it not have been much more convenient if we only had one? Why could someone not get them together and produce just one volume, with each writer contributing their part?

This may seem a logical and sensible approach, but something important is lost whenever people attempt to harmonize the Gospels into one volume. God had a good reason for inspiring four Gospels, just as he had a good reason for duplicating other parts of Scripture. For example, there are two accounts of creation in Genesis 1 and 2 – one from God's viewpoint, one from man's. And there are two accounts of the history of Israel in Kings and Chronicles, written from completely different perspectives although covering the same time period. In the same way we have four accounts of Jesus' life and death because God wanted to give us a number of **different angles** in order for us to grasp the full picture.

If you wanted to take photographs to show someone the shape of the aeroplane Concorde, you would have to take at least four or five, otherwise they would never understand the whole concept because it looks so different from every angle. Similarly Jesus is the most amazing character who ever lived and so God inspired four people to look at him for us and to write down what they saw. The writers of the Gospels each wrote independently, with their own perspective on Jesus.

INSPIRATION

This perspective on how the Gospels came to be written shows us something important about the inspiration of Scripture. It underlines that the writers of the Bible were not 'word processors', writing words dictated directly from the mouth of God.* God intended to use individuals who could bring their own understanding of Jesus and convey his message with a particular aim in view. Yet at the same time, what they wrote is no less the Word of God, each word being inspired. It is both the words of man and the Word of God. Inspiration therefore includes the individuality of each author.

How are the Gospels different from one another?

When a famous figure dies there is typically a series of different types of writing which follow his death.

1. The first publications usually tell us **what the person did**; early obituaries fulfil this aim.
2. Later people become more interested in **what the person said**, and so begin to publish collections of letters and speeches.
3. Then comes the third stage, which looks behind the words and deeds to discover **what the person was**, examining character, motivation and what they were really like.

The four Gospels follow these three stages quite markedly, as the table on pages 10–11 demonstrates. Mark is most concerned with what Jesus did, focusing on his actions, miracles, death and resurrection. Matthew and Luke both include far more about what Jesus said, recording more of his preaching

---

* Some parts of Genesis and Revelation are an exception to this and bear the marks of having been given directly in verbal form.

than Mark does. John, however, is not just interested in what Jesus did, nor does he focus on what he said. His supreme concern is with Jesus' identity, with who he was. While the Gospels are distinctive as forms of literature, they do encompass a wide range of reflection on Jesus, providing an all-round view and giving the reader a comprehensive understanding.

How to study the Gospels

Having noted the distinctiveness of the Gospels as a form of literature, there are two levels on which we can approach them in order to unlock their meaning. The first has already been indicated, namely the need to examine each Gospel from the point of view of the **writer's insight**, looking at what he saw and understood about Jesus from his angle. The other is to look at the Gospel in terms of the **writer's intention** and how he wanted readers to respond. The two levels overlap, but will help us enormously when we come to look at each book.

The writer's insight

Each Gospel writer wanted to convey a particular insight about Jesus and so organized his material accordingly (see the table on pages 10–11). He wanted to do more than just convey remembered words and deeds of Jesus – he also wanted to give a context in which the life of Jesus could be understood. His viewpoint is not necessarily unique to his Gospel: there is overlap between the writers, but it is clear that each writer has a primary insight.

- Mark wrote the first and shortest Gospel, seeing Jesus as the Son of Man.
- Luke wrote the second Gospel and saw Jesus as the Saviour of the World.

- Matthew wrote the third Gospel, depicting Jesus as the King of the Jews.
- John wrote the fourth Gospel, with Jesus as the Son of God.

The writers chose and structured their material in the way that would best convey their particular perspective.

The writer's intention

However, we also need to consider each Gospel from the point of view of the reader. Each writer has a particular audience in mind and is concerned to convey his message about Jesus to them.

Careful study indicates that Matthew and John are written for believers:

- Matthew is concerned for new believers and his book is arranged in order that we will know how to live as disciples.
- John is written for older believers, to encourage them to hold on to their faith in Jesus and also to counteract heresies about John the Baptist and Jesus himself.

On the other hand, Mark and Luke are written primarily for unbelievers.

- Mark is concerned to excite his readers with the news about Jesus so that they might have faith in him.
- Luke, as the only Gentile author in the Bible, is concerned that fellow Gentiles might know about Christ.

The different audiences govern what the writers include and how they arrange their material.

Similarities

We have already noted that there is overlap between the Gospels' content and their wording, with the first three being especially similar. In fact, 95 per cent of Mark is included in Matthew and Luke, in some cases with very similar or identical wording. These first three are known as **'synoptic' Gospels**. The word 'synoptic' is made up of two Greek words, *syn*, which means 'together', and *optic*, which means 'see' or 'view'. The first three Gospels reflect a common view of Jesus, as opposed to John, who writes more independently. There is an enormous change when you finish reading Matthew, Mark and Luke and start reading John.

Much material is common to all three Gospels. A few things are found only in Mark, but both Matthew and Luke used most of his material, though in different ways. Matthew split Mark into little bits and mixed these up with his own material, whereas Luke took blocks of Mark, using whole chunks at once.

Of course there has been some debate: did Matthew and Mark use Luke, or did Matthew and Luke use and expand Mark, or did Mark abbreviate Matthew and Luke? It is most likely that Matthew and Luke expanded Mark, working with his Gospel in front of them. Matthew has some material which is unique to him, which he did not get from anyone else, and Luke also has some of his own.

MARK AS THE BASIS

Not surprisingly, the three synoptics have a clear literary connection, based on Mark. Although placed second in our New Testament, Mark was almost certainly written first. He divides his Gospel very carefully into two parts with an interval in between. The first covers Jesus' ministry in the north, in Galilee. The second part covers Jesus' move south to Judaea.

Apart from one incident in Nazareth when the villagers tried to throw him off the cliff, Jesus was very popular in the north, where thousands followed him. But he was very unpopular in the south, where he had frequent problems. The Jewish authorities were hostile, and few followed him. With this division, Mark builds up to a climax as Jesus leaves the friendly north for hostility and eventual death in the south.

This two-part framework is one that Matthew and Luke both use as their basis. Luke is the next Gospel to be written. He rewrites Mark, adding both his own material and other content common to Matthew. This probably comes from a separate source, written or oral, known to both Matthew and Luke, and designated by New Testament scholars as 'Q' after the German word for 'source' (*Quelle*). Matthew then composed his Gospel, adding material from his own research, including material from 'Q', but arranging it differently to suit his own particular purpose.

Conclusion

If we are to grasp its message fully, it is important that we understand what a Gospel is and for whom it is written. The table below summarizes what has been said about the Gospels.

FOUR GOSPELS
Mark – Son of Man
Matthew – King of Jews
Luke – Saviour of the World
John – Son of God

THREE STAGES
What Jesus did – Mark
What Jesus said – Matthew/Luke
Who Jesus was – John

TWO ANGLES
Writer – insight
what? how?
Reader – intention
who? why?

In the Gospels we have four news bulletins, conveying to us the person and work of Christ, with unique first-hand accounts of his life and times, written with the purpose of building up believers or convincing non-believers to put their faith in the one whom God has sent. They are best read through in one sitting, preferably aloud, as they were preached before they were written down.

They are extraordinary books, for they describe 'the hinge of history'. The world will never be the same again. Christ has come, a man yet at the same time God, to be the Saviour of the world. Because of this, time has been divided into two epochs: BC (before Christ) and AD (*anno domini*, Latin for 'year of our Lord').

PART I

MARK

Introduction

We saw in the general introduction to the Gospels (pages 9–10) that Mark was the first of the four to be written, although it is placed second in our New Testament. It is written primarily for **unbelievers**, and you quickly notice its vivid, dramatic and emotional style. It is a gripping page turner, hard to put down once started.

Who was Mark?

The author of Mark's Gospel, like the authors of the other three Gospels, does not name himself. He refuses to draw attention to himself, although there are clear hints telling us who the writer is. It is almost as if he is saying that he wants the whole of our attention to be on Jesus, not on him.

He is a man with three names, each giving a clue to his background.

1. 'Mark' comes from the Latin name **Marcus**, telling us that although he was Jewish he did have official Roman connections in some way. We do not know for sure what these were, but his family had quite a big house in Jerusalem and must have been of some standing, with at least one maidservant.

2. His Hebrew name was **Johannan**, or John, which means 'Yahweh (God) has shown grace', and he was often known as John Mark.
3. His third name is unusual: **Colobodactolus**, a Greek name which means 'stubby fingered'. The first Gospel ever to be written was by someone with stubby fingers!

So Mark had three names, a Greek nickname, a Latin name and a Hebrew name.

HIS FAMILY HOME

Mark's mother was Mary, which is Miriam in Hebrew. There is a strong possibility that his family home was the location of the Last Supper. This is understood because of an unusual incident following Jesus' arrest in the Garden of Gethsemane, directly after the Last Supper which took place in an 'upper room' in Jerusalem.

We read that as Jesus was arrested the soldiers grabbed hold of a young man who was dressed in nothing but a bed sheet. He struggled clear, leaving the sheet in a soldier's hands, and fled naked into the night. This is an unusual detail to include unless this was John Mark himself, who had left his house in a great hurry to follow the disciples into the Garden, then had hidden behind one of those old olive trees, heard Jesus praying and saw his arrest. It would explain how we know the details of Jesus' prayer, which took place out of earshot of the disciples he had taken with him.

This is speculation, but it is very likely that the location of the Last Supper was John Mark's home and that this incident provides support for his authorship.

How did he get his information?

John Mark was not part of the apostolic band. As a youth he would have seen Jesus, but he was never a leading figure in the unfolding events. Although he is mentioned elsewhere in the New Testament, it is always as a 'number two', someone's personal assistant. So it is perhaps surprising that of all people John Mark should write the first Gospel.

He was personal assistant to three very great Christian leaders in the early Church and this gives us a clue to his source material. First he assisted his older cousin, **Barnabas**, a Levite from Cyprus. It would seem that Barnabas trained him in Christian service.

Next, Mark became an assistant to the apostle **Paul**, accompanying Paul and Barnabas on their first missionary journey. It was not a complete success, with John Mark backing out when they reached the coast of Asia Minor. Luke does not record for us in Acts exactly why he left. Maybe he was homesick. Some speculate that he struggled to accept Paul's leadership because he felt that his cousin Barnabas should have been the leader. Others suggest that the dangers of attack from bandits put him off. We do not know for sure. We do know, however, that when Paul and Barnabas set out on their second journey, John Mark became the focus of an argument, with Paul insisting that John Mark be left behind following his previous desertion and Barnabas arguing that he should come. In the end Paul and Barnabas parted company over this.

Finally, Mark became personal assistant to the apostle **Peter**, who arrived in Rome after Paul. It was from this relationship that Mark received the information for his Gospel. His initial task was to act as interpreter for Peter's messages, translating them into Latin as Peter travelled around the churches in Rome. An early Church document tells us that some members of the congregation of the church in Rome asked if they could have Peter's sermons recorded in a more permanent form. They were afraid that Peter's boldness would lead to his arrest, especially as this was the time of the feared Emperor Nero, and they were anxious that his memories of Jesus should not be lost. The record says that Peter was not especially enthusiastic about the idea, but that 'he neither hindered nor encouraged Mark to do this'.

Style

As a result of his close connection with Peter, the Gospel of Mark has also been known as the '**Gospel of Peter**'. Indeed, a close examination of Peter's sermons in Acts reveals a close correlation with Mark. Peter's own temperament shines through the pages of this Gospel. We could nickname him 'Action Man', since he was so impetuous, frequently speaking before thinking and often prepared to act when others were more cautious. We know from other Gospels that Peter was the one who wanted to walk on the water. He was the one who grew tired of waiting for Jesus to appear after the resurrection and said, 'I'm going fishing.' He was the one who jumped into the water when John said it was Jesus on the shore.

Peter could not sit still and this Gospel conveys this breathless excitement throughout. The word 'immediately' comes many times, summing up Peter's zest for life. For this reason Mark's Gospel is the most vivid and the most alive of the four and the most exciting to read aloud. The actor Alec McCowen packed a London theatre for months with a simple recital of Mark's Gospel.

In the first part of Mark relatively little time is spent on the first two and a half years of Jesus' ministry. It is written in a fast-moving style as Mark seeks to excite the reader with what is happening. But in the second part he spends more time on subsequent months, then even more time looking at Jesus' last weeks, until he focuses right down on the last week and the last day, when every hour is described. It is like an express train slowing up and coming to a halt – and it halts right in front of the cross.

In his structure Mark is building everything up towards Jesus' death, and slowing everything down to stop before the cross. It is a masterly piece of journalism, and is probably the best Gospel to give to a complete outsider who knows nothing about Jesus and wants to read about this exciting person who is our Saviour and Lord.

The content of Mark's Gospel

Peter's weaknesses

Mark's Gospel typically places Peter in a bad light, for there is far more emphasis on his weaknesses than his strengths – almost as if Peter was concerned that readers should know about his **mistakes**. So Mark includes Jesus' words to Peter: 'Get behind me, Satan!' when he protests against Jesus' explanation of his future suffering. By contrast, in Matthew we read, 'You are Peter, and on this rock I will build my church and the gates of Hades will not overcome it.' Mark also includes the moving account of Peter's denial of the Lord, but fails to include his reinstatement, which appears in John.

Miracles

Peter was far more impressed with **what Jesus did** than what he said, and so the Gospel displays a great enthusiasm for Jesus' miracles. This reflects an evangelist's heart, keen on anything which would interest unbelievers in the message. This is borne out by the relative proportions of Mark devoted to the miracles and the discourses. Mark includes 18 miracles, which

is similar to Matthew and Luke. He includes only four parables, however, compared to 18 in Matthew and 19 in Luke, and
only one major discourse, in Chapter 13.

Omissions

Peter's own ignorance is also reflected in the Gospel. It
would seem that Peter did not know how or where Jesus was
born. Never once in his speeches in Acts or in his letters does
he indicate any knowledge whatever of Jesus' birth. Peter's
knowledge began at the River Jordan, where he and his brother
Andrew were baptized and John introduced them both to
Jesus. In Mark, therefore, there is no Christmas story or tales
about Jesus' boyhood. The Gospel gets going where Peter's
knowledge began – with John preaching and baptizing.

Shape

The Gospel covers the three years of Jesus' public ministry, but
its shape is reflected in both time and space, **chronology** and
geography. The narrative builds up over the first two and a
half years to a watershed moment (see below, pages 22–4), and
then everything flows down from that, covering the last six
months of Jesus' life on earth. Mark focuses on Jesus' Galilean
ministry, omitting his visits to Jerusalem in the early years. (See
diagram overleaf.)

CHRONOLOGICAL STRUCTURE

There are three phases in the ministry of Jesus.

- **The first phase**: Jesus was very popular. Thousands came to
  be healed and he was the talk of the whole country.
- **The second phase**: The opposition begins. Starting with a
  difference of opinion over the Sabbath, it extended to other
  areas and soon Jesus had made more enemies than friends.

■ **The third phase**: Jesus concentrated on his 12 disciples, out of the thousands who flocked to hear him.

The Gospel covers three distinct periods of time. The first two and a half years are covered in Chapters 1–9, Chapter 10 covers the next six months, and Chapters 11–16 cover Jesus' last week.

GEOGRAPHICAL STRUCTURE

The geographical structure of the Gospel parallels the time divisions. The story starts at the River Jordan, which is the lowest point on the earth's surface, and moves from there to Galilee, where Jesus conducted the bulk of his ministry. The diagram indicates an ascent up to the highest point in the Promised Land, Mount Hermon, at the foot of which is the town of Caesarea Philippi. It is here that the Gospel reaches its **watershed**. As soon as that point is reached Jesus sets his face towards

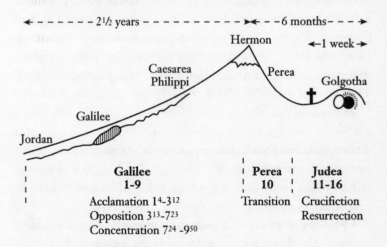

Jerusalem and it is downhill all the way – literally down from that high point to Judaea, through Perea, which is on the east side of the Jordan, and eventually to Jerusalem, where Jesus dies on the cross and rises again three days later.

So what happened at Caesarea Philippi after the first two and a half years that changed the direction of Jesus' ministry so totally, and which Mark is so keen to highlight for his readers?

THE WATERSHED MOMENT

A little background will help us. Caesarea Philippi is located at the source of the River Jordan, which emerges at the foot of Mount Hermon and measures 30–40 feet in width. The source of the water is the snow on the top of Mount Hermon, which melts and filters down a crack inside the mountain, flowing out through a hole beneath the actual surface of the river.

This strange natural phenomenon became the focus for superstition and religious cults and the centre of pagan worship for centuries. In the cliff face above the river there are carved alcoves, in which were placed statues of gods. One statue was of the Greek god Pan and to this day the place is called Paneas or Baneas. There was also a statue of Caesar, put there by one of Herod the Great's four sons, Philip, who was given that part of the land when Herod died. Philip called the place after himself and after the Roman Emperor, hence the name Caesarea Philippi.

So here we have a statue of the Greek god Pan, a god who was supposed to have appeared on earth as a mortal man, and a statue of Caesar, a man who was called a god. It was to this location that Jesus took the 12 disciples and asked, 'Who do people say I am?'

The disciples replied with the various views of the day: mostly reincarnations of great men from their history – Jeremiah, Elijah, even John the Baptist.

Then Jesus asked them pointedly who *they* thought he was. It was Peter who had the right answer. He realized that Jesus had lived before, but not down here on earth. '**You are the Christ**,' he said.

This was the first time that any man had grasped who Jesus was (the first woman was Martha, whose confession is recorded in John's Gospel). It is this answer which is the pivotal point in the Gospel. Jesus had waited two and a half years to ask the question, and now he was able to talk to Peter about two things he had never mentioned before:

1. He spoke about being able to **build his Church**, a subject never mentioned before, even amidst all his preaching, healing and miracles. The reason is evident: Jesus cannot build his Church until people know who he is, for the Church can only be made up of people who know his identity. At this point Jesus renames Simon (which means 'reed') and he becomes Peter. The name is a play on words, for 'Peter' is very close to the word for 'rock' in the original language, as in our word 'petrified'.

2. He also spoke for the first time of his **intention to go to Jerusalem and die on the cross**. The disciples had been with him for two and a half years and he had never before given a hint that he was going to die. Now he explains that he must go to the cross and nothing will stop him. Peter is alarmed and announces that he must not go, only to be rebuked by Jesus. From this point on, the cross is the focus for the Gospel.

This, then, is the **watershed** of Mark's Gospel. We can easily miss the real flow and development of the story if we do not realize this, assuming things about the disciples because we know how they turned out, but missing the progressive revelation portrayed in the Gospel.

Now that the disciples have understood who Jesus is, the next incident follows on quite naturally. Jesus takes Peter, James and John up to the top of the mountain, above the snow line, where he is transfigured before them. In describing the event, Peter says that Jesus' clothes became brighter than any bleaching agent on earth could make them. He actually uses the word 'detergent' (or 'fuller', which was the equivalent in those days). The light was shining through Jesus' clothes from the inside and they 'saw his glory'. He met with Moses and Elijah to discuss his 'exodus', whereby he would accomplish a release for his people, as Luke records.

The key point of the Gospel, therefore, is the realization by the disciples of who Jesus is: he is the Christ, the Messiah. This is the key point for the readers too. This is the **good news** Mark is communicating through the shape of his Gospel. It is picked up by Matthew and Luke, who then build on it.

Mark's value to us

1. A clear picture of the person of Christ

Mark is primarily concerned with what Jesus did, but he is not unconcerned about the person of Christ. Indeed, it is Mark who makes it clear that **Jesus revealed himself to his followers gradually**. It is a puzzling feature of a Gospel that reveals the person of Christ that it also highlights the fact that Jesus himself seemed to want his identity kept quiet.

A number of references emphasize this point most markedly.

- In 1:25 and 1:34 Jesus would not let the demons speak because they knew who he was.
- In 1:43, having healed a man with leprosy, Jesus sent him away at once with a strong warning: 'See that you don't tell this to anyone.'
- In 3:12, again speaking to demons, 'he gave them strict orders not to tell anyone who he was'.
- In 5:43, having raised Jairus' daughter to life, 'he gave strict orders not to let anyone know about this'.
- Other incidences along the same lines occur in 7:24, 7:36, 8:26, 8:30, 9:9 and 9:30. Even on Mount Hermon Jesus asks his disciples to keep quiet about his identity.

This special feature of Mark is known as the 'Messianic secret' and reflects Jesus' concern to complete his mission without interruption. He wanted the disciples to understand from his Father who he was, and he restrained their thinking so that they would arrive at the conclusion the right way. He also kept his identity hidden because early recognition of his Messiahship would lead to premature adulation and a demand that he become a political messiah, which would hinder his ministry and could conceivably prevent his death.

2. Teaching on the work of Christ

The second great theme of Mark's Gospel is the work of Christ. He emphasizes the **death of Jesus**: one-third of the Gospel is concerned with the cross – a fact often lost on those who make plays and films about Christ's life. This underlines how unusual a Gospel is as a form of 'life story'. We could scarcely imagine the writings on famous public figures like Mahatma Gandhi or John F. Kennedy giving so much attention to their deaths, in spite of their assassinations.

The cross dominates the content throughout the Gospel. It is clear from Mark that people plotted to kill Jesus from the very beginning. He made enemies as well as friends through his teaching. His challenges to the religious status quo were unpopular with the religious and political leaders and aroused considerable hostility. The Pharisees in particular hated his attacks on their traditions.

HUMAN AND DIVINE ASPECTS OF JESUS' DEATH

Mark's emphasis on the cross includes both the human and the divine aspects of Jesus' death.

Human

On the human side, **Jesus was charged with blasphemy for saying that he was God,** which in Jewish law was a capital crime deserving death. We are told, however, that the accusers could not agree on the words he had used in order to confirm the validity of such a charge. Eventually the judge asked Jesus himself who he was. Of course, Jesus as a Jew had to speak when questioned by the High Priest, so he acknowledged that he was the Christ. The judge tore his clothes and said, 'You heard it! What is your verdict?' and the Sanhedrin, the ruling council of 70 men, said that he deserved to die.

Despite this verdict, they could not officially put someone to death, since the land was occupied by the Romans and was under Roman law when it came to the death penalty. They needed the Romans' approval for the death sentence, therefore, but in Roman law blasphemy was not a crime. The only hope was to *change* the crime and by the time Jesus came before Pilate he was being charged with **treason,** not blasphemy. It is Mark's Gospel which is the clearest on this point. In the end the offence they charged him with was not that he said, 'I am God' (blasphemy), but that he said, 'I am king, the king of the Jews' (treason).

The human side of the death of Christ was unjust from beginning to end. Although he was guilty of neither blasphemy nor treason, that is how he was charged and condemned.

Divine

The divine side of Christ's death, however, is also brought out in Mark, for **Jesus was sure from the very beginning that he had come to die**. He predicted his death, and his resurrection, more than once. We also read of Jesus taking the 'cup', an image which – used metaphorically – always speaks of God's wrath against sin. Mark no doubt heard Jesus use the word in the Garden on the night of his betrayal.

From the time that Jesus first mentions his future suffering, we have the sense that he had to be betrayed, that God had planned it that way, Jesus was aware of it, and there was no avoiding it. Peter must not try to tempt Jesus to run away from the cross.

This combination of the human and the divine is most compelling, confronting readers with the stark realities of Christ's mission. It makes this a very suitable Gospel to give to unbelievers.

3. People's reactions to Jesus

Mark frequently records people's reactions to the teaching and miracles of Jesus. There are two key words all the way through – **fear** and **faith**. From beginning to end of the Gospel, it is as if those who meet Jesus are faced with a choice between the two. Mark seems to be asking: What is your response to this story, fear or faith?

In the account of the stilling of the storm, for example, Jesus is in the boat and the disciples ask him, 'Don't you care if we drown?' Jesus answers, 'Why are you so afraid? Do you still have no faith?' One of his favourite sayings given throughout the Gospel is, 'Don't be afraid.' Fear and faith are incompatible responses to any circumstance or situation.

A basis for belief

In Mark's Gospel, therefore, we are presented with a clear picture of the person and work of Christ, and an encouragement to respond in faith rather than fear when the supernatural element enters in. These are further reasons why Mark is such a good Gospel to give to unbelievers. It gives them a very basic knowledge of Christ's person and his work, and encourages their right response to both.

The ending

Mark's Gospel has a very peculiar ending. It actually **finishes in the middle of a sentence**. In the early manuscript copies we have of the Gospel it ends right in the middle of verse 8 in Chapter 16, with the strange phrase 'for they were afraid of...' English translations usually tidy up the language with 'for they were afraid' or 'they feared'. But nothing can hide the fact that the Gospel ends suddenly, and ends with this note of fear.

Reasons for the ragged ending

That the Gospel should end in this way is surprising, as Mark's whole theme is to get people switching from fear to faith, and it raises a series of important questions: What happened to the rest of the story? Why is Mark not nicely rounded off? Why are there no accounts in Mark's Gospel of the appearances of Jesus after his resurrection? There is only the empty tomb and the finding of that empty tomb, but there is no mention of Jesus actually meeting the disciples, which is very strange when it is compared to the other three Gospels.

There are at least three possibilities to explain all this.

1. Mark **intended** to finish on this uncertain note and to leave the ending open.
2. Mark was **prevented** from finishing – i.e something interrupted his writing. He may have been suddenly arrested or taken off, or perhaps he dropped dead, and the manuscript was never completed.
3. The ending has been **lost** in some way. Either the manuscript was mutilated by persecutors, or it is even just possible that *Peter* tore the end off! As this is really 'Peter's Gospel', it is meant to be a record of his preaching about Jesus. We know from 1 Corinthians that one of the most important resurrection appearances was to Peter on his own, but we have no record of this in the Gospels. Maybe it was originally included by Mark, but Peter wanted it removed because he thought it was so precious, so intimate and so personal that he did not want any account of it to be published. Some argue that although we do not have the actual ending to Mark's Gospel, much of it is included in Luke and Matthew's versions anyway, as they drew so heavily on Mark's work.

We do not know what happened, but argument 1 is highly unlikely, for it would mean that Mark deliberately ended in the middle of a sentence, with the words, 'the women said nothing to anyone, for they were afraid of...' This would be an extraordinary ending for a Gospel intended to convey *good* news, especially one directed at unbelievers.

Another ending added

What we do know is that other endings have been added, both a shorter and a longer version. Somebody else has completed Mark's Gospel so that we do have the complete story.

The long version, which is the one usually included in Bibles today, runs from verse 9 to verse 20, and balances fear with faith – though it does tell us that the disciples did not believe Jesus had risen even when they saw him. It includes some remarkable statements by Jesus, many of which are not appreciated by sections of the Christian Church today. Jesus talks about tongues (the only recorded instance where Jesus mentions that his followers would speak in tongues), and says that his followers would cast out demons, heal the sick, and pick up snakes and not be harmed (which happened to Paul in Malta). There is also a statement here in which Jesus makes baptism in water essential to salvation. He says, 'Whoever believes and is baptized will be saved'.

We do not know who wrote this ending, but it does reflect what the early Church believed about Jesus' actions between his resurrection and ascension, and it includes items from the other Gospels. There is a little bit about the road to Emmaus and a short section similar to Matthew's Great Commission. It seems as if somebody has picked out various elements from the other Gospels, put them together and rounded off Mark that way. We need not worry about the authenticity of the longer ending. It is a valid part of the Word of God and does reflect the early Christian understanding, even if it does not deliver Mark's actual words.

Conclusion

The Gospel of Mark focuses on what Jesus did, as Peter conveys his appreciation of his master and is keen that non-believers should come to faith in him. It presents the basis for belief in a clear and vivid way. The Gospel also has significant value for those who are already followers of Jesus, reminding us of Christ's person and work, and of the need to respond to this 'news bulletin' with faith and trust. Its fresh and enthusiastic tone is a good antidote for those whose Christian walk has become stale because they have lost the wonder of the Christ event. Being the shortest, it is the easiest Gospel to read in one sitting. If you can, read it aloud for the best effect – either to yourself or, better still, to someone else.

PART II

MATTHEW

Introduction

Who was the writer?

It is commonly agreed that the author of this Gospel was Matthew, also known as Levi, although his name does not appear on the original document. His name means 'gift of God' and he was one of the twelve apostles. He was a tax collector at Capernaum and the Gospels of Matthew and Luke both record that he left everything to follow Jesus, and threw a party so that his friends and colleagues could meet Jesus for themselves. Although one of the Twelve, he is not one of the more prominent and is rarely mentioned in any of the Gospels.

How was the Gospel written?

We have already noted that Matthew was written using the content and framework of Mark's Gospel. There are considerable similarities, including identical wording in some places. Matthew follows Mark's broad arrangement of two distinct phases, whilst adding his own distinctive structure. So he includes 'phase one', the two and a half years in which Jesus ministers in Galilee, and 'phase two', the final six months in the south amongst the more nationalistic Jews of Judaea. He also sees the watershed of Christ's ministry coinciding with

Peter's confession of Christ at Caesarea Philippi and the subsequent movement of Jesus towards the south and the cross.

We have also noted the importance of getting to grips with the *writer's insights* – what he saw and understood about Jesus from his particular point of view – and with Matthew these can be highlighted by asking why he felt he needed to rewrite Mark. It is in examining the differences between his Gospel and Mark's Gospel that Matthew's purpose becomes clear.

The differences between Matthew and Mark

Insights

Matthew was one of the Twelve, and had time to reflect on the three years he spent living close to his master. While Mark stresses his humanity (the Son of Man), Matthew sees Jesus as the **King of the Jews**, the one who fulfils the promises of the prophets. No one had been on David's throne for 600 years – the current King Herod had no ancestral claim to it. Now at last one was coming who would be the rightful king.

From the very beginning Matthew focuses his readers' attention on Christ's ancestry in the royal line of David, describing how his birth fulfils prophecy and has the marks of God's involvement, heralded by archangels and welcomed by an angelic choir. While Luke includes the shepherds, it is Matthew who records the worship of the child by wise men from the east. This theme of Jesus as the King of the Jews is also seen in his passion, as Matthew records the crown of thorns, the 'sceptre' and the title given to Jesus, all mocking his pretensions – but to Matthew appropriate for a royal person.

Intentions

Matthew writes for a completely different audience from Mark. Mark is written for unbelievers, Matthew for **new believers**, many of whom at that time were converted Jews.

His intentions can be seen clearly at the end of the Gospel, where he records Christ's final words to his apostles, commanding them to 'make disciples of all nations'. Matthew certainly fulfils that aim, providing a manual of discipleship for those who enter the kingdom. Indeed, this was how the Gospel came to be used within the early Church and is one of the reasons why it is included first in our New Testament.

While Mark's Gospel was appropriate for someone interested in Christ but not yet persuaded, therefore, Matthew's rewrite of Mark accomplishes a very different purpose.

An earlier start

Matthew starts his account much earlier than Mark, with the birth of Jesus set in the context of his ancestry. Mark starts with his baptism and is less interested in, or even ignorant of, his birth. Thus well before we hear Jesus' teaching and see his miracles, Matthew has set the scene for us, creating a sense of expectation as the Jewish messiah arrives on the scene of history.

A longer account

Matthew is the fullest and most systematic account of Jesus' life, reflecting perhaps the orderly mind of an accountant. He includes material from his own observations as one of the Twelve, as well as some research of his own. Both Luke and Matthew apparently use a common source unknown to or ignored by Mark. Not only does Matthew add the birth of Jesus, he has more discourses and collected sayings, and more detail concerning Christ's death, with 14 extra sayings of Jesus included in the narrative of his death.

Alterations

Matthew has made a number of alterations to Mark's text in order to bring out aspects he feels are important. Matthew's accounts are often shorter, omitting harsh or vivid detail to produce a smoother story which clarifies any misunderstandings and spares the blushes of the disciples. The 'feel' of Matthew therefore is more sober, less enthusiastic and less emotional than Mark. This is an older man reflecting on his own first-hand experiences, and he comes across more as a teacher than a preacher.

Collected sayings

Matthew collects the sayings of Jesus into five 'sermons' (see the table below), forming summaries of his teaching on discipleship. The Sermon on the Mount is best known, but there are four others on the connected theme of the **kingdom**. This is by contrast to Mark, who has very little in the way of discourse, and to Luke, who spreads the sayings of Jesus all the way through the narrative.

Given the Jewish readership, it is highly likely that Matthew has a special reason for presenting exactly *five* sermons. Their place at the heart of his Gospel parallels the five books of the law of Moses which begin the Old Testament (Genesis to Deuteronomy). Matthew is telling his readers that Jesus brings a **new law** – not the law of Moses any more, but the law of Christ. Hence throughout the Sermon on the Mount we have Jesus' restatement of the law: 'You have heard it said in the law of Moses, but I say to you...' Things will never be the same again.

Structure

Matthew uses Mark's basic framework, as we have already noted, but he adds his own structure. Alongside the two-phase division of Mark he adds two motifs prefaced by the phrase 'From that time…' So we read, 'From that time on Jesus began to preach, "Repent, for the kingdom of heaven is near",' and 'From that time on Jesus began to explain to his disciples that he must go to Jerusalem and suffer many things…' The first appearance of the phrase captures the sense of his ministry in the north, and the second the inevitability of his death in the south. Matthew also uses the words, 'When Jesus had finished…' to change direction in his narrative.

The most marked and telling structural change, however, concerns the way in which he alternates the five blocks of Christ's teaching with four blocks of his deeds. We can lay this out as follows:

THE STRUCTURE OF MATTHEW

Introduction: birth, baptism, temptation

Word	Chapters 5–7
Deed	Chapters 8–9
Word	Chapter 10
Deed	Chapters 11–12
Word	Chapter 13
Deed	Chapters 14–17
Word	Chapter 18
Deed	Chapters 19–23
Word	Chapters 24–25

Conclusion: death and resurrection

So we have five sermons, four of them followed by accounts of the deeds of Jesus which serve to illustrate his sermons. The purpose for this will be examined in more detail later, but for now we should simply note that Matthew is keen to demonstrate that Jesus communicated in word *and* deed, giving us a model to follow. Mark invites us to come and see what Jesus did, but Matthew invites us to come and see what he did *and* hear what he said.

Narrative on the cross

Matthew has a considerably fuller ending than Mark. In view of Mark's abrupt ending, some have speculated that the last part of Matthew may actually have been Mark's original ending. We have no way of knowing, but can list his particular distinctives in the last two chapters.

1. **Details of the arrest**: Matthew is concerned with Christ's innocence, so he emphasizes that these things happened so that Scripture might be fulfilled.
2. **The end of Judas**: Matthew records the warnings of Jesus to the disciples and the remorse of Judas as he returns the money, though by then it is too late.
3. **Events immediately after Jesus died**: It is Matthew who records the opened tombs and the sightings of previously dead people in the city of Jerusalem.
4. **The tomb**: Matthew records the guarded tomb and the report by the soldiers that the body was stolen.
5. **After the resurrection**: Matthew says much more than Mark about events following the resurrection. He records Jesus' return to Galilee, and his meeting with the 11 disciples (and about 500 others, some of whom 'doubted'). There is great significance in the location. Galilee was at the crossroads of the world, with Mount Megiddo a crossover point where roads from the east, north, south and west converged. The population here was cosmopolitan, 'Galilee of the nations'. Jesus was on a mountain, reminiscent of Moses on Mount Nebo. It is at this point that

the Great Commission is given: they must make disciples
of all nations (literally all ethnic groups).

The special features of Matthew

A. His interest in Jews

As well as drawing on Mark for material, Matthew adds a number of special features of his own, and the reader is immediately struck by the Jewishness of Matthew's Gospel. It is obviously
aimed at Jewish readers, though not exclusively so. His sensitivity to Jewish concerns and interests can be seen throughout.

1. GENEALOGY

The Gospel begins with a genealogy, of little interest to
Gentiles but fascinating for Jews keen to know about **Jesus'
ancestry**, for in their mind the family tree establishes the person. Furthermore, the arrangement of the genealogy alerts
Jewish attention. Jesus' ancestors are arranged in three groups
of 14, the first group from Abraham to King David, the second
from David up to the exile, and the third from the exile to
Jesus. These periods represent the eras when God's people
were governed by a particular style of leadership: prophets,
princes (kings) and priests.

The significance of the three groups may be lost until we
realize that every Jewish name has a numeric value, with each
letter assigned to a number and the total forming the number
of the name. David in Hebrew (which has no vowels) is DVD
and comes to 14. So immediately we see Matthew's concern to
convey a pattern: Christ's ancestry is Davidic, and he has come
at just the right time.

Matthew chooses to give the genealogy of Joseph's ancestors. We may think there's nothing unusual about that – until

we recall that Jesus was not *physically* related to Joseph. Why not follow Luke in giving Mary's ancestry? Because to a Jewish mind it was the *legal rights* that mattered, and they came through the father.

One further point of interest is that a Jew carefully versed in his Old Testament would note that if Jesus was a *physical* descendant of Joseph, his rights to the throne of David would be questioned, since Jeconiah is listed as one of Joseph's ancestors. God had said through Jeremiah that no descendant of Jeconiah (also known as Jehoiachin) would ever sit on David's throne. Matthew's purpose was to establish Jesus' *legal* claim to be a 'son of David'.

2. TERMINOLOGY

Matthew's sensitivity to Jewish readers is further seen in the language he uses. Most marked is his reference to the 'kingdom', a key theme of Jesus' message. Matthew writes of the **'kingdom of heaven'**, not the 'kingdom of God' as in the other Gospels. Jews would avoid using God's name in speech for fear of speaking irreverently and so Matthew uses the phrase 'kingdom of heaven', even though his meaning for the phrase is the same as for the phrase 'kingdom of God' used by the other writers.

3. OLD TESTAMENT USE

Matthew refers to the Old Testament more than any of the other Gospels. One of his favourite sayings is 'that it might be fulfilled, which was spoken by the prophets'. This is one of the reasons why Matthew is placed first in the New Testament, even though it was not written first. It provides **continuity** with the Old Testament better than all the others. Altogether there are 29 direct quotations from the Old Testament and an additional 121 indirect references or allusions.

This is seen in particular in Matthew's birth narrative. He seems to Gentile eyes to take a long time explaining why Jesus was born in Bethlehem – because the prophets had predicted that Bethlehem of Judaea would be the birthplace of the king. Yet this would be crucially important for Jews wondering if this was the Messiah God had promised long ago. Matthew is keen for readers to understand that the prophets spoke of the birth to a virgin, the flight to Egypt, the return to Galilee and the slaughter of innocent infants. The phrase 'that it might be fulfilled, which was spoken by the prophets' occurs 13 times in the story of Jesus' birth, where Matthew quotes Micah, Hosea, Jeremiah and Isaiah.

4. MESSIAH

In addition, Jewish readers would have a particular problem believing that Jesus was the Messiah in the light of his **crucifixion**. How could the Messiah be condemned as a criminal and sentenced to death? So Matthew stresses that Jesus was actually innocent of all the charges. It was the Jews who were guilty of unjust accusation, illegal trials, and changing the charges in order that the Romans might convict and execute him. Matthew spells out why the Jews did not receive their Messiah and includes a list of woes against the Pharisees, the most religious of all Jews.

5. THE LAW

Linked with the Jewish emphasis is Matthew's concern that we understand the law correctly in the light of Jesus' teaching. Matthew emphasizes as no other Gospel that Jesus did not come to abolish the law, but to **fulfil** it. Matthew records the words of Jesus, that 'not one jot, or one tittle of the law will pass away'. Many Jews thought Jesus had come to destroy the law, but Matthew states clearly that this was not his purpose.

He came that it might be 'fulfilled' – achieved rather than annulled.

WHY WOULD MATTHEW WRITE SO STRONGLY FOR THE JEWS?

To keep the door open for Jews

By the year AD 85, just after Matthew wrote his Gospel, Jewish believers were being excommunicated from the synagogues. The Church as a whole was becoming more and more Gentile. Consequently a deep gulf was opening up between the Jews and the Church. Matthew wanted to keep the door open for Jews, to help them realize that the followers of Jesus were not abandoning the Old Testament, nor had they forgotten their Jewish roots. He was a Jew, they were his people and, like the apostle Paul, Matthew had a longing that Jews should come to believe in their own Messiah.

To remind Gentiles of their roots

Secondly, Matthew wrote a Gospel that was Jewish in character because he wanted Gentile Christians never to forget their Jewish roots. Matthew, more than the other Gospels, roots Jesus in Judaism, putting him in the context of God's purposes for Israel, with a genealogy reaching back to Abraham and David.

He is saying to Jews on the one hand, 'Don't run away from Christians,' and to Christians on the other hand, 'Don't run away from Jews.' This Gospel intends to bring Jew and Christian together.

B. His interest in Gentiles

Matthew's purpose is not exclusively Jewish. He is careful to mention **Christ's concern for Gentiles** too.

- At the very beginning wise men from the east, possibly Gentiles, come to see the baby in Bethlehem.
- In the genealogy of the first chapter, Ruth and Rahab, both Gentiles, are listed.
- We are told that Jesus ministered in 'Galilee of the Gentiles'.
- Matthew records the faith of the Roman centurion, hailed as extraordinary by Jesus.
- We read of people of the east and west coming to sit in the kingdom.
- The gospel is good news to the Gentiles who will trust in his name.
- We read of the Canaanite woman's faith.
- Matthew records that Jesus is the cornerstone rejected by the builders and that the kingdom will be taken away from the Jews and given to the Gentiles.
- At the end of the Gospel Jesus commands his followers to go and make disciples of all 'nations', and the word he uses means all the ethnic groups, i.e. Gentiles.

Furthermore, Matthew does not hesitate to record the **negative words Jesus used when referring to the Jews**. He includes a whole chapter devoted to 'woes', as well as other scattered comments. A 'woe' was a curse word. Chapter 23 is a collection of his sayings against the Pharisees and religious leaders. It is stern stuff.

We tend to be rather more keen on the blessings, forgetting that Jesus uttered curses as well. In Jesus' day there were 250,000 people living on the shores of Galilee in four major cities. Today there is just one town. Why? Jesus said, 'Woe to you, Chorazin ... Woe to you, Bethsaida ... and you, Capernaum...', and they have all disappeared. The only town he never cursed was Tiberias and it is still there.

C. His interest in Christians – Jewish or Gentile

A MANUAL FOR DISCIPLESHIP

We have seen already that Matthew wrote his Gospel with new converts in mind, and that his purpose can be gleaned from Jesus' command at the very end of the Gospel, when he leaves his followers with a job to do before he returns: 'Go and disciple all ethnic groups, baptizing them and then teaching them to observe everything I have told you to do.' These words provide the basis for our understanding of Matthew's aim: **to help disciples** by teaching them what Jesus commanded. We might call his Gospel a 'manual for discipleship'.

It is by far the best book of the New Testament to give to new converts. It is carefully designed to teach them how to live now that they are disciples of Jesus. The Christian life may start with a *decision* for Jesus, but it takes years to make a *disciple*. A key element in discipleship is learning **how to live in the kingdom of heaven on earth**, and Matthew wrote his Gospel precisely for that purpose: so that we could make disciples.

THE CHURCH

Such a purpose explains why Matthew is the only Gospel to record Christ's words about the Church. The word is used in two very different senses – the **universal Church** and the **local church**.

The first use comes following Peter's confession that Jesus is 'the Christ, the Son of the living God', a key turning point in the Gospel. Once his followers had realized who he was, Jesus could build his Church. And having built his Church, he could die on the cross. Here the word 'church' refers to the universal Church, the whole Church of Jesus. There is only one Church of Jesus Christ and he is building it.

The second meaning of the word comes in Chapter 18: 'If your brother offends you go and tell him. If he repents of it you have won your brother. If he refuses to admit he was wrong, take two or three witnesses. If he still refuses to confess it tell it to the church'. This cannot mean the universal Church, but rather the local community of which the offended person is a part.

In these sayings Matthew outlines the two meanings of the word 'church' in the New Testament: there is the Church of Jesus, which he is building, and the local church, which is part of that universal Church and to which you can take your complaints when necessary.

Not only is Matthew the only Gospel to speak of the Church, it is also clear that some of the teaching is specifically intended for the later age of the Church, post-Pentecost. Matthew records teaching which was not immediately relevant to its hearers. For example, of the 37 verses in Chapter 10 dealing with Jesus' instructions to the Twelve, only 12 verses were immediately relevant. The chapter speaks of Gentile persecution, but at this stage Gentiles were not involved in any persecution, so Matthew is including material from the lips of Jesus which was specifically meant to be of *future* relevance. Similarly, the 'church' discipline of Chapter 18 must have been given for a later period, since the disciples could not have understood it at the time.

THE KINGDOM

If teaching on the Church is unique to Matthew, his teaching on the kingdom covers themes also included in the other Gospels. But 'the kingdom' is a *particular* interest of Matthew. None of the other writers give it the same prominence. We saw earlier that he arranges Jesus' teaching into five blocks. These are all on kingdom themes. Furthermore, his parables often commence with the words, 'The kingdom of heaven is like...' This dominant theme reflects the preaching of Jesus

and is one which runs through the whole story of the Bible as
God sets about the re-establishment of the kingdom of heaven
on earth. It is, of course, a theme that unites both Jew and
Christian as both look for the kingdom of God. This fits in
with Matthew's aim of uniting Jew and Gentile.

There is, however, a crucial difference between the *Jewish
expectancy* of the kingdom and the *Christian experience* of the
kingdom, which explains why so many of the Jews failed to
understand that Jesus was their Messiah. It is important to
understand this if we are going to grasp Jesus' teaching on this
theme. (See diagram below.)

To the Jew the kingdom is wholly future – it is something
that has not yet come and therefore they call it 'the age to
come'. Today, when the Jewish nation celebrates the Feast of

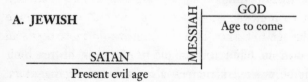

A. JEWISH (Israel)	**B. CHRISTIAN** ('Church')
Quotations	Gentiles
Allusions	Disciples
Explanations	
Compilations	
(5x = 'law' of Christ)	**Manual of Discipleship**

KINGDOM OF HEAVEN (= God)

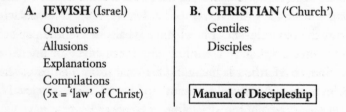

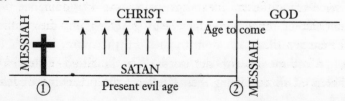

Tabernacles every September or October, they look expectant-
ly for the coming Messiah to bring the kingdom of heaven here
on earth. That is the centre of their hope. They see the present
time as the 'present evil age', the world being ruled by Satan.
The devil is the prince of this world, the ruler of this world, the
god of this world. These are titles which both Jesus and Paul
gave Satan, but they were already familiar titles to the Jewish
people.

The difference in the Christian hope for the future is this:
**Christians believe the Messiah has already come, but also
that he is due to come again.** In Matthew Jesus speaks of this
as the secret of the kingdom, namely that the Messiah is coming twice, not once. So the 'age to come' which the Jews look
for has already begun – it has broken in with Jesus. The kingdom of heaven has come in a very real sense and is now here,
but it overlaps with the 'present evil age', rather than replacing
it as the Jews expect. Between the two visits of the Messiah the
two ages overlap. The reason why Christians are in tension
is that we are living in the 'overlap of the ages'. The kingdom is
both now and not yet, inaugurated but not consummated. Not
yet established, it can still, however, be entered now.

With this understanding of the *coming* kingdom we can
better understand why the message of the Gospels was such
an affront to Jews who thought they were all good enough
to enter the age to come. John the Baptist told them they had
to get cleaned up and be baptized in the Jordan, so that their
sins might be washed away, ready for the coming kingdom.
Many were completely oblivious to the need. Once we grasp
this very different idea concerning the kingdom, we will
understand much better the teaching of Jesus and the conflicts
he encountered.

Matthew is keen that the theme of the kingdom should be
balanced appropriately with other teaching, for this focus on

the kingdom – with believers as subjects of the king – can lead us to think of our relationship with God solely in those terms. The frequency with which a word is used is often a key to a writer's emphasis, and Matthew mentions 'Father' 44 times altogether, compared to just 4 times in Mark and 17 times in Luke. He is stressing that as we live as subjects of the King of Heaven, we can also call him 'Abba, Father'. We are sons as well as subjects. If we were merely subjects seeking to obey a king, we could start to think that our obedience somehow saves us and forget the filial relationship into which God calls us. So this is a powerful antidote to legalism and a life based on rules and regulations.

Given the understanding of the kingdom outlined above, it is possible to identify the main theme of Matthew's Gospel as this: **How do you live in the kingdom now?** Let us take a brief look at the five 'sermons' into which Matthew has gathered Jesus' teaching about the kingdom.

1. The lifestyle of the kingdom (Chapters 5–7)

This compilation is better known as 'the Sermon on the Mount' and is often badly misunderstood. It is not Jesus' advice to non-believers on how to live. It is tough enough for a believer to seek to live this way, never mind a non-believer. No, the sermon teaches us **how believers are to live, now that they are in the kingdom**.

It starts with a remarkable series of statements: 'Blessed are the poor in spirit, for theirs is the kingdom of heaven ... Blessed are the meek, for they will inherit the earth ... Blessed are the pure in heart, for they will see God...' Jesus is describing a new kind of person, a changed character.

After the opening 'beatitudes', the commands in the sermon are wide ranging and intensely practical. Here are just a few examples:

■ If you have called somebody an idiot, you are a murderer.
■ The law of Moses said, 'Do not climb into bed with a woman you are not married to,' but Jesus says, 'Do not even look at a girl and wish you could.'
■ He also says, 'Do not divorce and remarry.'
■ We are told not to worry, for if we worry we libel the King of Heaven, who looks after his own creation and so will look after us.

This is the lifestyle of the kingdom and these chapters provide excellent material for someone who is recently converted. The vital point to grasp is that they are not saved *by* but *for* such a lifestyle.

2. The mission of the kingdom (9:35–10:42)
This 'sermon' follows logically on from the first. Matthew indicates that when a person enters the kingdom they have a mission to go and bring others in. A large amount of Jesus' teaching on **evangelism** therefore comes in Chapters 9 and 10.

Jesus instructs his disciples to demonstrate the reality of the kingdom by raising the dead, casting out demons and healing the sick, and then to tell those who have observed that the kingdom is coming. So the *actions* should precede the *words* about the kingdom. The passage also gives considerable detail about how they should travel, what they should take and how they should respond to opposition.

3. The growth of the kingdom (13:1–52)
We move next from mission to growth. What should we expect concerning the **spread of the kingdom**? Here the teaching is through a series of parables.

- The sower: we should not worry if three out of every four seeds come to nothing. From the one seed in good ground you can get a yield of 30-, 60- and 100-fold, so it will be worth it.
- The wheat and the tares growing together: the kingdom of Satan will grow alongside the kingdom of God, until they are separated at the final harvest.
- The grain of mustard: Jesus describes a seed which becomes a big tree, depicting the growth of the kingdom from very small beginnings and paralleled accurately by the growth of the Church. Jesus started with 11 good men and now has 1,500 million!
- The pearl of great value: we are told how to value the kingdom, for it is like a precious pearl. We should be prepared to give up all we already have in order that we may possess it.
- The net: Jesus tells us not to worry about bad converts, because the kingdom of heaven is like a net which is full of all kinds of fish, both good and bad. His message is that we must wait until the 'fish' are finally brought to shore on the last day, rather than trying to sort them all out as soon as we have caught them.

4. The community of the kingdom (18:1–35)

Matthew includes here some of the teaching Jesus gave concerning the **relationships of those within the local church**. He speaks of how we should deal with those who drift away from the faith, and how we should handle those who sin against others within the community of believers.

5. The future of the kingdom (Chapters 24–25)

By the time Matthew wrote his Gospel, many Christians were asking when Jesus would be returning. So Matthew (as do Luke and Mark) includes a section helping his readers to know what they should look for by way of **signs of his coming**.

The location for this 'sermon' is significant: Jesus and the disciples are sitting on the Mount of Olives overlooking the temple and the disciples are asking Jesus about the end of the age. Matthew links the disciples' questions about this with Jesus' prophecy that one day the temple would be destroyed.

Jesus gives them four signs to look for before his coming:

1. Disasters in the world: wars, famines, earthquakes, false Christs.
2. Developments in the Church: universal persecution, falling numbers, false prophets, completed mission.
3. Danger in the Middle East: sacrilegious dictator, unequalled (but limited) distress, false Christs and false prophets.
4. Darkness in the sky: sun, moon and stars gone, sky-wide lightning, the coming of the true Christ and Christians gathered 'from the four winds'.

Of these four signs, the first is already to be seen; the second is well on the way; the third has yet to appear, and when it does the fourth will immediately follow.

Matthew continues the section with a series of parables focusing on being ready for the King when he gets back. In every parable there is the phrase 'he was a long time coming', emphasizing the need for faithfulness in the face of considerable delay.

MAJOR THEMES

We have seen already a number of themes which are part of Matthew's particular concern. There are three others which we also need to consider, all of them fundamental to discipleship in the kingdom.

1. Faith

The first that comes up repeatedly is the theme of faith. It is not unique to Matthew, but is certainly a special interest of his. His message is that a subject of the kingdom who is also a son of the Father lives by faith. This does not refer to a one-off decision of faith, but to someone who, having believed, goes on believing. Often in Matthew, Jesus asks people, 'Do you believe what I have told you? Do you believe that I can do this?' Jesus looks for a **continuing trust** in him and in his Word. He reserves his highest commendation for the centurion who came to him for healing, contrasting his great faith with the lack of faith in some parts of Israel.

2. Righteousness

One theme which you will not find in the other Gospels is that of righteousness – the need for **doing as well as believing**. It is made quite clear that the order is important: you believe first, but you believe in order to do. Take one of the shortest parables in the whole Gospel, for example, about a man who had two sons and asked them to go and work in his vineyard. One said 'yes', but did not go; the other said 'no', but went. Jesus went on to ask which of the two did the will of his father, implying that we can profess to be obedient, but we lie when we do not actually do what he tells us. Being a disciple is not just believing in him but actively 'doing righteousness'.

This is made clear in many places in Matthew's Gospel. It is the underlying reason for the baptism of Jesus, and explains the meaning of it, which is often misunderstood. Why was Jesus baptized? He had no sins to wash away, nothing to be cleansed, and yet he came to John to be baptized. When John protested that it was Jesus who should be baptizing him, Jesus still insisted, because 'it is right for us to fulfil all righteousness'. It was not an act of repentance for him as it was for everybody else, but it was an act of righteousness. His Father had told him to do it, so he did it. At the very start of the Gospel, Jesus demonstrates the importance of doing by modelling himself the very activity he would expect from his followers.

It is not surprising, therefore, that his teaching is full of this theme. He says that, 'unless your righteousness exceeds the righteousness of the Scribes and Pharisees, you will not enter the kingdom'. The Pharisees were a group who were excessively religious. They fasted twice a week; they gave tithes of all they possessed; they traversed sea and land to make proselytes; they were great missionaries; they read their Bibles; they prayed. And yet Jesus said that the righteousness of his followers must exceed all that.

Just as it is important that we understand exactly what is meant by faith, so we must make sure we come to terms with the concept of righteousness as Matthew presents it. Jesus is not saying that we are saved *by* righteousness, but that we are saved *for* righteousness. It is an important distinction. If Matthew's Gospel is given to an unbeliever, they may get the impression that being a Christian means doing good, but in fact it is *after* you become a Christian that – having been saved and forgiven – you are able to display the righteousness of doing as described in Matthew.

3. Judgement
This third theme may seem surprising: it seems to contradict the thesis that Matthew wrote a Gospel for believers. Yet there is in Matthew a considerable volume of teaching on judgement from the lips of Jesus himself. What is more, a close examination of the context of each warning about hell will reveal that all but two were given to born-again believers.

Matthew is **warning disciples against complacency**. Starting to follow Jesus is no ticket to heaven. Followers must fear hell themselves if they are to remain 'on the way'. So while two of the warnings of judgement are given to the Pharisees, the rest are directed at those who had left all to follow Jesus. Most strikingly, he never warns sinners in this way.

This truth becomes especially clear when we consider the context of one of Christ's most famous statements about hell: 'Do not fear those who can kill your body and after that do nothing; rather fear him who can destroy body and soul in hell.' Who is he talking to? He is actually addressing Christian missionaries (the Twelve) just before he sends them out to declare and demonstrate the kingdom. He does not say that the fear of hell should be part of their message to sinners, but rather that they should fear it themselves, for when they fear hell, they will not fear anyone or anything else, even martyrdom.

If we had only the Gospel of Matthew in the whole New Testament we would have enough to know that Christians should fear finishing up on God's rubbish heap, which Jesus called 'Gehenna', the valley of Hinnom outside Jerusalem where everything useless was thrown to be burnt up. Matthew is a sobering Gospel for disciples, teaching them to be serious, to press on, to go on believing, and to go all the way with Jesus.

HOW MATTHEW'S MESSAGE IS TAUGHT

Given Matthew's aim of providing a discipleship manual, we might ask why he put all this teaching into the framework of Mark's Gospel. Why did he not just call it a manual for discipleship and record the teaching which a disciple needs? The answer to this question gives a profound insight into the way Jesus and Matthew intended that their hearers and readers should learn.

Context

Matthew is being true to the way the teaching was originally given by Jesus. Jesus gave his teaching in the context of his deeds and he performed his miracles in the context of his teaching. Teaching needs to be given in this practical context. We need the **balance of word and deed**.

A two-way process

We also need to be told the *indicatives* of the gospel: **what Christ has done for us**, and then be faced with the *imperatives*: **what we are to do for the Lord**. We are led astray if we focus on one and not the other. If we concentrate on what God has done, we might imagine that we need do nothing, and this can lead to licence (i.e. how I live does not matter). If we focus only on what we do for the Lord, we might imagine that it is all down to us, and this can lead to legalism (i.e. my works earn my salvation). Instead, our behaviour needs to follow from our belief – we work out what he works in. The power of the kingdom releases us from sin so that we may live in the purity of the kingdom. The kingdom is both an offer and a demand. So what God does for us and what we do for him are all part of the gospel, the good news of the kingdom.

The need to balance the indicative and the imperative is especially true when we consider the cross of Christ, for it is particularly dangerous to divorce Christ's teaching from all that he achieved there. We cannot teach people how to live the Christian life *without* giving them the teaching in the framework of what Christ achieved for them on the cross. Matthew's order helps us to be continually grateful to Jesus for all he has done. He wisely decided to present the disciples' teaching in the framework of the good news that the Jesus who demanded all this from his followers was the Jesus who healed the sick, raised the dead, and died and rose again for us.

Conclusion

Matthew's Gospel was a firm favourite with the early Church. They were concerned with the Great Commission, to go into all the world and make disciples of all nations, teaching them to observe all that Jesus had commanded. Matthew's Gospel enabled them to do just that, as a manual of discipleship for both Jewish and Gentile believers, uniting the Old and New Testaments and telling the world that the Christ has come, the King of the Jews, fulfilling the promise to Abraham that through him and his seed all the nations of the world would be blessed. Here is the son of David come at last – and here is how we should live today as subjects of the King.

LUKE AND ACTS

Introduction

The Bible is made up of the words of man and the Word of God – many human authors but one divine editor. Most of the authors were responding to an immediate need and had no idea that what they were writing would one day be part of the Bible. We can therefore study the books of the Bible at two levels: the historical and the existential. On the historical level we ask: Why was it written? What was the human reason behind it? On the existential level, we ask: Why is it in our Bible? Why does God want us to know about this? This will be our method as we consider both the Gospel of Luke and the book of Acts later on. The two books have the same author, and together they make a rather special case. So who was Luke and why did he write these two volumes?

Who was Luke?

1. A GENTILE

Luke is unique amongst all the authors in the Bible because he is the only Gentile. His 'English' name comes from the original Loukas and he was a native of Antioch in Syria, which was the Paris of the ancient world at the eastern end of the Mediterranean Sea, well north of the Promised Land.

It was at Antioch that the first Gentile church was established and the followers of Jesus Christ were first called 'Christians' – a somewhat disparaging nickname given to them by the locals who noted that they sought to follow 'Christ'. While this name has become popular today and has a wide range of definitions, in Acts the words 'believer' or 'disciple' were commonly preferred.

Luke was well placed as a Gentile to show through his writing how the gospel spread from Jerusalem to Rome. We can easily forget that it is a unique thing for a religion to jump ethnic barriers, especially from being essentially Jewish to becoming largely Gentile. Most people are born into their national religion and stay there. Here is a religion which has jumped from one people to another. This focus on Gentile readers is demonstrated in a number of ways. For example, Luke avoids the Hebrew and Aramaic expressions 'rabbi' and 'Abba' used in Matthew and Mark, preferring to translate such words into Greek for his readers, to make sure that they understand.

2. A DOCTOR

Luke was a doctor by profession – the apostle Paul refers to him as 'the beloved physician' when writing to the Colossian church. Medicine had been developing for 400 years and doctors received careful training. Luke needed to be observant, analytical and careful in his records – skills which he also uses in writing his Gospel and the book of Acts.

There are many incidents which betray Luke's medical background. The birth of Jesus, for example, is told from Mary's angle. We have the details of Jesus' circumcision, mention of the swaddling clothes or diapers – all the kind of things a doctor would be interested in. (Incidentally, Luke gives us Mary's genealogy to trace Christ's physical ancestry, while

Matthew gives us Joseph's line.) When Mark describes the sickness of Peter's mother-in-law he calls it simply a fever; Luke writes of a 'high fever'. Of the miracles which Luke records, five out of six are miracles of healing.

God uses a doctor to report the supernatural! The virgin birth, the miracles of Jesus, and the signs and wonders in the book of Acts all come from Luke's pen. Some doctors are sceptical about anything which is outside the natural, physical realm, but Luke is able to bring his considerable skill as a writer and physician to record what actually took place, even when it was outside medical knowledge or ability.

3. A HISTORIAN

Luke was meticulous in his detail, wording and grasp of cultural nuances. Not an apostle himself, he was dependent for his knowledge of Jesus on those who were close to him. Some modern historians have criticized his writing, claiming that he was mistaken, but subsequent archaeological findings have always found in favour of Luke, to the point where he is now recognized as one of the finest historians of his day. Indeed, if we treat 'Gospel' as a different genre from 'history', as suggested earlier (page 4), then Luke is the only *history* writer in the New Testament. His primary objective was to provide an accurate and reliable account of what had been said and done in the life of Jesus, rather than announce the good news of salvation, though there was bound to be an overlap between the two.

4. A TRAVELLER

Luke was also a very experienced traveller. It is Luke who refers to the 'Sea' of Galilee as a 'lake' – it is only 13 kilometres long and 8 kilometres wide. To a seasoned traveller, this would certainly be merely a lake! He travelled with the apostle Paul, indicated by the so-called 'we' passages in Acts. Luke remains anonymous, similar to other New Testament writers, seeking to divert attention away from himself, but the use of 'we' betrays the fact that he was there. Luke was Paul's travelling companion, especially when Paul was at sea – on the voyage from Troas to Philippi, Philippi to Jerusalem, and Caesarea to Rome. Maybe Paul felt the need of a physician when he sailed? Some of Luke's finest writing depicts the voyages towards the end of Acts and the eventual wreck on the shores of Malta.

This willingness to travel is a significant factor in our understanding of how Luke's Gospel and Acts came to be written. We know that Paul was under arrest for two years in each of two places – in Caesarea and Rome. We will see later that it was probably during these times that Luke composed his two-volume work – the Gospel in Caesarea, and Acts in Rome, where of course he could interview Paul at his leisure.

5. A WRITER

Luke writes in an educated, polished Greek similar to that of Hellenistic historians. His skill as a writer will be examined when we consider Luke and Acts in more detail (see pages 85–6). His account of the shipwreck in Malta has been acclaimed as one of the masterpieces of literature from the ancient world. He has a good vocabulary, an excellent style, and an ability to hold the reader's interest, with a smooth and speedy switch from one plot to the next. His skill as a historian is also evident; his research is thorough and he knows what to include and what to leave out.

6. AN EVANGELIST

Luke was an evangelist – with his pen rather than his voice. 'Salvation' is a key word in both books. That word and its cognates are used repeatedly. As a Gentile Luke is especially concerned that salvation comes to 'all flesh'. In his Gospel he records John the Baptist's quotation from Isaiah, 'and all flesh shall see the salvation of God', and many have seen this as the key theme of the Gospel of Luke.

We will see later, in our study of the Gospel, how Luke has particular interest for various groups of people who can and will see the salvation of God. Similarly, the theme of Acts is the Holy Spirit poured out on all flesh – on Jews, on Samaritans, unto the ends of the earth. This 'Jewish' religion is for everybody in the whole wide world: Luke portrays Jesus as the Saviour of the world.

History records that Luke died at the age of 84 in Boeotia in Greece, having never married.

The audience

Having looked at the writer, let us turn now to the audience he was writing for in his two-volume work. Luke wrote these volumes for one man, Theophilus, which literally means 'Mr God-Friendly'. It seems strange that he should spend four years researching in order to write for just one person, even if he did think there might be a wider audience one day. Who was this man Theophilus?

One theory is that Theophilus is a fictional figure, just as an author might write a book for an imaginary representative of a group – 'Dear Mr Sincere Enquirer'. So Theophilus is a made-up name, 'God-Friendly' meaning somebody who is interested in the faith and wanting to find God. However valid the theory, however, it does not fit all the facts.

Others argue that he was a real person, probably a publisher interested in Christianity – an intriguing idea, certainly. It is indeed better to see Theophilus as an individual who really did exist. He was obviously a man of some importance, in some public office, because Luke gives him a title as well as a name: 'Most Excellent' Mr God-Friendly. This is precisely the same title used for Festus and Felix when they presided over Paul's trials, strongly suggesting that Theophilus was in the legal profession, either a lawyer or a judge. Why, though, would Luke want to give a lawyer such a full account, first of Jesus and then of Paul?

Paul's defence lawyer

If we imagine that Theophilus is Paul's defence lawyer, or even his judge at the trial in Rome, then it becomes clear. Either would need to have a full brief, detailing the circumstances leading to the trial.

How did this new religion start? Who was the founder? How did Paul come to be part of its propagation? Furthermore, the lawyer would be especially interested in how this faith was viewed by the Roman authorities. So when Paul was imprisoned in Caesarea, Luke researched the life and death of Jesus, and when Paul was moved to prison in Rome, he did all the research and recording of Paul's contribution to this new religion.

His work includes traces of him having interviewed a number of people we know to be important in the New Testament Church: James, probably Matthew, and certainly John (there are some things in Luke that are only otherwise found in John – for example, he and John are the only two to record the cutting off of Malchus' ear during the arrest of Jesus).

Compilation of the books

Luke had certain disadvantages when it came to collecting the necessary material for the 'defence brief'. He was not one of the Twelve, he had never met Jesus, and he was not an eyewitness of his life and ministry. But he overcame these difficulties by visiting those who *were* eyewitnesses. He collected the accounts about Jesus while he was waiting for two years in

Caesarea until Paul was shipped to Rome. When Paul arrived in Rome, there were another two years during which Luke could write up the story of Paul in his second volume, the 'Acts of the Apostles'.

If the notion of the 'defence brief' is correct, it would explain so much in both volumes. It would explain why the Romans are portrayed as entirely sympathetic to this new religion throughout the two books. Both in the trial of Jesus and in the trial of Paul, Luke includes three statements that the men are totally innocent. Pilate says three times that Jesus is innocent, and three times Roman authorities say Paul could have gone free if he had not appealed to Rome. So in both volumes the trouble surrounding the Christians is not caused by Romans, but by Jews seeking to cause problems for this new faith.

Eyewitnesses

A lawyer would require first-hand testimony, eyewitness accounts, and **carefully researched facts** presented in an orderly fashion. Both of Luke's volumes include careful dating by Roman events (e.g. Luke 2:1 and 3:1) and his introduction to Theophilus in his first volume confirms his purpose: 'Many have undertaken to draw up an account of the things that have been fulfilled among us, just as they were handed down to us by those who from the first were eyewitnesses and servants of the word. Therefore, since I myself have carefully investigated everything from the beginning, it seemed good also to me to write an orderly account for you, most excellent Theophilus, so that you may know the certainty of the things you have been informed about.' This wording certainly fits in with the type of material a lawyer would require.

FOCUS ON PAUL

This theory also explains the unusual features of the second volume. Acts is known as the 'Acts of the Apostles', but it centres on just two of them, barely mentions others and omits any reference to the majority. In addition, while Peter is the main character in the first 12 chapters, he disappears almost as soon as Paul is converted. The book then focuses almost exclusively on Paul, accounting for two-thirds of the account. This would seem an unusual proportion, unless the whole work was primarily intended to defend Paul and explain to the Roman authorities that there was nothing seditious or subversive about the new religion. Paul is thus depicted as a Roman citizen, innocent by Roman law and deserving a 'not guilty' verdict at his trial.

There is also an interesting difference to be noted from Jesus' trial in Jerusalem. He was innocent by Roman law, yet was crucified because of Jewish pressure. Paul, by contrast, is on trial in a place where the Jews could not influence the verdict. His appeal to Caesar precluded their interference.

It explains too why Paul's testimony is given three times in the book of Acts – a little excessive (none of the other apostles give their testimony) unless it is because Paul is on trial and it is vital that the lawyer hear what he said at every one of his previous trials, so that all of it can be used in evidence for him and not against him.

In addition, seeing Acts as a defence lawyer's brief helps explain why Acts finishes so abruptly. It stops with Paul awaiting trial. This also discredits other arguments for the purpose of Acts. If it was purely an account of Paul's life, this would be an odd place to finish. We know that Luke himself lived to the age of 84, so he was alive to record Paul's death if that had been his purpose with Acts. If, on the other hand, the purpose was legal, then the brief finishes as we would expect, with Paul awaiting trial.

One final anomaly could clinch the matter. Why would Dr Luke give so much space to such a detailed account of the shipwreck on Malta if he was aiming to write a history of the early Church? And why would he describe only this disaster at sea, since Paul had been through at least three others? Surely it was because he wished to highlight Paul's exemplary behaviour in not attempting to escape in the confusion, but instead saving the lives of all on board, including his Roman captors, who were responsible for delivering him safely to the Roman court. After recounting this heroic and patriotic effort, I can imagine the defence lawyer at Paul's trial concluding with the words, 'I rest my case, your honour.'

WAS THIS BRIEF SUCCESSFUL?

All the evidence points to Paul being acquitted at his first trial in Rome. The letters he wrote to Timothy and Titus contain details which do not fit into his life before that and so imply that he was freed. There is even a strong tradition that he achieved his ambition of reaching Spain. Some of the ancient churches in Spain claim that Paul was their founder.

We cannot say for certain, but the evidence of tradition points to the fact that Paul was released at his first trial, but later re-arrested and then beheaded. Despite that ultimate outcome, it looks as if Luke's work was not wasted: if he wrote the two volumes primarily to save Paul's life in that first trial, and thus free the apostle for more ministry, then he succeeded.

Conclusion

We have focused here on Luke's concern for Paul, but it is also clear that the trial had repercussions for Christianity everywhere. It was not just Paul but *Christianity* that was on trial: what happened in Rome spread everywhere, so this was an important test case.

Luke's two volumes could be called *The History of Christianity, Parts 1 and 2*. They comprise a superbly written account covering a period of 33 years, from the beginning of Jesus' public ministry through to Paul's imprisonment or house arrest in Rome. It is full of unique information, so that the original reader and also later readers would know for sure what took place and how they should respond.

Luke was doubtless aware that his work would interest a **wider audience** too, with the general public in Rome becoming aware of the amazing spread of Christianity. Soon it would no longer be seen as a sect of Judaism, but as an advancing, universal and international faith, and it was becoming important news in Rome itself. Luke's work, therefore, was not just a defence brief, but a **declaration of the faith** and as such was a crucial contribution to the mission among the Gentiles.

His Gospel, therefore, is a piece of unique material. In the opening he tells Theophilus that many others have drawn up accounts of what happened. He would have known about Mark, maybe Matthew and possibly other records. But his own Gospel is the fruit of **wide-ranging, original research**, including interviews and verbatim accounts from eyewitnesses, all set within the context of the Roman world. He portrays the wide vista and then zooms in to focus on individuals. Despite the fact that Luke was not himself an apostle, there was never any doubt that Luke–Acts should be included in the New Testament 'canon'. That is truly a mark of how the early Church regarded this outstanding work, 'apostolic' in content and authority if not in authorship.

PART III

LUKE

Introduction

Luke is the best loved but the least well known of all the four Gospels. This may seem a surprising observation. Most people know the parts **unique** to Luke extremely well: the parable of the Good Samaritan is a favourite of many, with the very words now included in our language; most people know what is meant by 'the prodigal returns' from the story of the 'prodigal' son; the accounts of Jesus meeting with Zacchaeus, Mary and Martha, the dying thief and the two on the road to Emmaus are also very familiar.

But where Luke's material **overlaps** with the other Gospels, we tend to know their accounts much better than his. For example, what is meant by the description of disciples as 'salt', recorded by Matthew and Luke? Most people assume that this refers to the work of the believer in being a preservative and a flavouring in society, taking the meaning from the uses of salt in food preparation. But Luke records further details, saying that if salt loses its saltiness it is fit neither for the soil nor the manure heap. This implies that the metaphor is actually to do with the land and not the kitchen. Salt came from the Dead Sea and was full of potash and other salts. It was used as a fertilizer in farming and as a disinfectant for human waste. As such, salt made good things grow and stopped bad things spreading: the disciples, Jesus said, should do the same. Most people fail to notice Luke's additional details and read their own meaning into Matthew's 'salt of the earth'.

Another example of our neglect of Luke comes in the saying, 'For if men do these things when the tree is green, what will happen when it is dry?' On speaking engagements I have often teased my hearers by taking a vote on whether they think this comes from the Old Testament, the New Testament or William Shakespeare. The majority are usually wrong! Actually, Jesus said these words as he carried his cross to Calvary. Only Luke records these words, which few seem to have read.

Elements unique to Luke

The structure of Luke's Gospel is based on Mark's arrangement, with the key watershed moment happening at Caesarea Philippi, after which Jesus made for Jerusalem. But it can also be seen as falling into five sections:

1:1–4:13	The first 30 years of private life
4:14–9:50	Galilean ministry
9:51–19:44	Journey to Jerusalem, with teaching greatly expanded
19:45–23:56	Last days in Jerusalem (this part is radically different from Mark's approach)
24	Resurrection and ascension

Let us consider the parts which are unique to Luke.

Birth stories

The birth stories are all from **Mary's angle**, in contrast to Matthew's focus on Joseph. It gives a very different feel to the narrative. Luke has more human interest and gives intimate details of the conception and delivery, even mentioning the swaddling clothes. Luke includes a genealogy of Jesus as Matthew does, but his is drawn from Mary's side and goes back further, to Adam. Legally, Jesus is a descendant of David through Joseph, but his physical descent is traced through Mary, also to King David. So Jesus is a royal prince twice over.

Luke's birth narrative also indirectly gives us the **month of Jesus' birth**. We are told that Zechariah belonged to the priestly tribe of Abijah. We know from 1 Chronicles which month this tribe was called on to serve in the temple: in the one-year cycle they were the eighth tribe out of 24. So Zechariah was there in the fourth month of the Jewish calendar. We know that Elizabeth became pregnant at that time, and that this was six months ahead of Mary, so we can calculate that Jesus was born 15 months later, in the seventh month of the following year at the Feast of Tabernacles (late September or early October to us). The Jews expected the Messiah to come at that feast and still look for him then to this day.

Boyhood story

Luke records the only story about the first 30 years of Jesus' life. At the age of 12 Jesus had his Bar Mitzvah, which means 'able to do good deeds'. When a Jewish boy reaches this age he becomes responsible for his own behaviour. Up to the age of 12 the parents are punished when the boy does wrong, but from then on he is responsible for his own behaviour and for keeping God's commandments. He is taken to the synagogue and he reads a portion of the law of Moses. From that time on he is considered a man. At that point he becomes a partner with his father in whatever trade or profession his father has.

This explains the story of **Jesus' visit to Jerusalem with Joseph and Mary**. In those days the women went ahead, walking 15 miles a day and then putting the tents up and cooking the meal for the arrival of the men. The children under 12 travelled with their mothers, and the boys over 12 travelled with their fathers. Jesus may have travelled there with Mary, as he had always done before, but as he was now 12 it would have been normal for him to have come back with Joseph. It is understandable that each thought Jesus was with the other.

It also sheds further light on the reply Jesus made when Mary found him in the temple. 'Didn't you know that I was in my father's house [or business]?' These are the first recorded words of Jesus. The most amazing thing is that it then says he came back to Nazareth and was subject to his parents. The story reveals that Jesus knew who he really was, even at the age of 12. It is also clear that Mary had never told him who he was (she refers to Joseph as 'your father').

Baptism

At the baptism of Jesus Luke also includes unique information. It is Luke who tells us that **Jesus received the Holy Spirit** after his baptism **as a result of prayer**. Matthew and Mark record him receiving the Spirit as he came up out of the water, but it is Luke who mentions his prayer: 'And as he was praying, heaven was opened and the Holy Spirit descended on him in bodily form like a dove.' Indeed, Luke tells us more about baptism in the Spirit than any other writer in the New Testament. This is a theme we will consider in more detail later (page 81).

The teaching of Jesus

UNIQUE TEACHING BLOCKS

Luke's treatment of Jesus' teaching is also different. Matthew's Sermon on the Mount becomes the Sermon on the Plain and every beatitude is matched with a woe. So, for example, 'Blessed are you who mourn' is coupled with 'Woe to you who laugh now'. This need not suggest that Matthew and Luke conflict in any way. It is clear that Jesus preached that sermon more than once and in varied forms. Luke has simply given us a very different and shorter form of the sermon.

UNIQUE PARABLES

A number of Jesus' stories we owe entirely to Luke:

- The parable of the good Samaritan
- The parable of the prodigal son (or rather prodigal father and two lost sons – see the paraphrase on pages 87–9)
- The parable of the persistent widow
- The parable of the Pharisee and the tax collector
- The parable of the friend at midnight, banging on a neighbour's door to get some bread for an unexpected visitor
- The parable of the barren fig tree
- The parable of the crooked manager
- The parable of Lazarus and the rich man who finished up in hell – the only parable to have the name of anyone in it ('Lazarus' may even refer to an actual person; see paraphrase on pages 91–2)
- The parable of the two debtors

UNIQUE INCIDENTS

Among the unique events are:

- The miraculous catch of fish
- The mission of 'the Seventy' (given as 72 in some versions)
- The ascension. This is the only Gospel to include an account of the ascension, apart from the brief mention in Mark's 'longer' ending, and Luke also records an account of it at the start of Acts, thus linking the two works and emphasizing the significance of this event.

Luke also includes particular incidents about **people** who especially interested him.

- The prostitute who anointed Jesus' feet in the house of a Pharisee
- The woman touching the hem of his garment in the middle of a big crowd
- The meal at the home of Martha and Mary
- The tax collector up a tree (Zacchaeus)
- The healing of the man with dropsy
- The crippled woman
- The ten lepers
- The widow's offering
- The dying thief
- The two on the road to Emmaus

These stories underline that Luke had more interest in people than any other Gospel writer – not an unexpected feature from someone who was a family doctor.

Interest in people

There are at least six groups of people in whom Luke had a special interest.

1. SAMARITANS

Samaritans were a group **regarded as outcasts by the Jews,**
because they were the result of Jewish intermarriage with
Gentiles during the exile. There was so much antagonism that
Jews travelling between Judaea and Galilee would make a longer
journey east of the Jordan rather than travel through Samaria.

Only Luke tells us that the one leper who returned to say
'thank you' after 10 were healed was a Samaritan. The rest
were Jewish, and they took the blessing of healing for granted.

Luke also records how James and John wanted to call down
fire from heaven on the Samaritans because they were rude to
Jesus. He then continues the story in Acts, where we read how
John comes back to Samaria with Peter, to pray that the
Samaritans might receive the fire of the Holy Spirit!

He also, of course, tells the story of the Good Samaritan,
'good' not being an adjective normally regarded as appropriate
for these people. In playing on the Jewish hearers' astonishment that such a person might be so caring, Luke reveals his
concern that this story of Jesus be preserved – as an encouragement to Samaritans, no doubt, and as an aid to healing the rift
between the two peoples.

2. GENTILES

As a Gentile himself, it is natural that Gentiles should figure
large in Luke's story, and the label itself is made prominent.
Luke betrays this theme early on, when Simeon says that Jesus
would be 'a **light to the Gentiles**'.

He records Jesus' mention of the widow of Zarephath and
Naaman the Syrian in his sermon at Nazareth. It was the
suggestion that these Gentiles had more faith than the people
of Israel that caused local people to attempt to take Jesus' life.

Luke also tells us of the sending out of the Seventy, a number which Jesus regarded as symbolic of the nations, based on

Genesis 10, and he includes the ministry of Jesus east of Jordan in Perea. The other Gospel writers include Jesus' journey from the north to Jerusalem, but omit the work he accomplished on the journey through non-Jewish territory.

3. OUTCASTS

Luke has a great interest in all outcasts, in **any people whom others treated with contempt**. He records the healing of the 10 lepers, and the calling of Zacchaeus the tax collector. This profession was despised on two counts: first because of the tax collectors' collusion with the Romans, who gave them the responsibility to collect the taxes, and second because their wages came from whatever they could acquire on top of the taxes themselves. Yet not only does Jesus meet with Zacchaeus, a member of this unpopular profession, but we are also told that on that day 'salvation' came to his house.

Luke also records the involvement of the shepherds in witnessing and broadcasting news of the birth of Jesus. In those days shepherds had a reputation for being untrustworthy parasites on society, living on what they could pilfer from others. As a result, a shepherd's testimony was not regarded as legitimate in a court of law.

It is also noteworthy how Luke includes the story of the exprostitute who anointed Jesus' feet, her model response to his forgiveness being an object lesson to the self-righteous.

4. WOMEN

Luke shows a particular interest in women. Martha and Mary have been mentioned already. In addition Luke writes of the woman touching the hem of Jesus' cloak, and the healing that then took place. No other writers comment on the women weeping for Jesus as he carried his cross. Furthermore, Luke names the wealthy women who supported Jesus' ministry financially. The Gospel includes **10 women who are not mentioned anywhere else** and another three in parables.

5. POOR

Luke seems almost **biased towards the poor**. For example, he records Jesus' words, 'Blessed are you who are poor' and 'Woe to you who are rich', whereas Matthew says, 'Blessed are the poor in spirit' and includes no reference to the rich. In Luke's Gospel poverty is seen as a blessing, in contrast to the way it was viewed by the people of Israel, who thought it was a sign of God's disapproval. He records that Mary and Joseph brought pigeons to the temple for sacrifice at the birth of Jesus. This was the cheapest possible sacrifice allowed under Levitical law.

He also includes a number of other sayings reflecting aspects of Jesus' teaching which touch on poverty:

- 'Give to everyone who asks you, and if anyone takes what belongs to you do not demand it back.'
- Jesus said to his host, 'When you give a luncheon or dinner, do not invite your friends, your brothers or relatives or your rich neighbours; if you do, they may invite you back and so you will be repaid. But when you give a banquet, invite the poor, the crippled, the lame, the blind, and you will be blessed. Although they cannot repay you, you will be repaid at the resurrection of the righteous.'
- At the parable of the great banquet: 'Go out quickly into the streets and alleys of the town and bring in the poor, the crippled, the blind and the lame.'
- In the parable of the rich man and Lazarus: 'The time came when the beggar died and the angels carried him to Abraham's side. In hell where he was in torment, he looked up and saw Abraham far away, with Lazarus by his side...'

6. SINNERS

The last category of people in whom Luke shows a special interest may seem surprising. But did Jesus not come to save sinners? A 'sinner' in those days was a special term for Jews who had **given up trying to keep the law of Moses**. There were 613 laws of Moses, which was hard enough, but the religious leaders had added even more. A high proportion of the population had just given up. Luke records stories and incidents highlighting that these were the very people Jesus had come to reach. He highlights how the Pharisees hated Jesus because he mixed with people who were not keeping the laws. How could he be close to God yet be so close to 'sinners'?

Luke is a very **humanitarian Gospel**. People mattered to Luke as they did to Jesus. He was concerned for those who could not help themselves, and whom others *would* not help. He was clearly fond of the word *splanknidzomai*, which means 'compassion', depicting Jesus as a man living not for his own power or popularity but so that the powerless might be touched by God. This is summed up in a statement at the end of the story of Zacchaeus: 'He came to seek and save the lost.' Similarly, we read: '...and the people all tried to touch him, because power was coming from him and healing them all'.

Other emphases in Luke

1. ANGELS

Luke has a particular interest in angels, especially at the start of his narrative. Heavenly beings announce the birth of John to Elizabeth, tell Zechariah what to name his son and announce the birth of Jesus to Mary. Then later, when Jesus is tempted in the wilderness, Luke records the ministry of angels, and as Jesus prays in Gethsemane we read: 'An angel from heaven appeared to him and strengthened him.'

It is said that members of the medical profession are the most sceptical about the supernatural. Luke the medic and careful historian not only sees no difficulty in including angels in his narrative, but is keen to stress their **vital role**.

2. THE HOLY SPIRIT

Luke has been called the '**charismatic Gospel**'. There is more about the Holy Spirit in Luke than in Matthew and Mark combined.

■ Luke records how the Holy Spirit is responsible for the conception of Jesus: 'The Holy Spirit will come upon you, and the power of the Most High will overshadow you.'

■ Both Elizabeth and Zechariah are said to have been filled with the Holy Spirit and it was prophesied that John the Baptist would be filled with the Holy Spirit within the womb.

■ The Old Testament concept of anointing by the Spirit is also seen in Anna and Simeon. Simeon is moved by the Spirit to meet the baby Jesus and Anna is described as a prophetess.

■ The Holy Spirit came upon Jesus at his baptism. Then we are told: 'Jesus, full of the Holy Spirit, returned from the Jordan and was led by the Spirit in the desert.'

■ After the time of temptation in the desert, 'Jesus returned to Galilee in the power of the Spirit...'

■ Luke records Jesus' teaching on praying for the Spirit: '...how much more will your Father in heaven give the Holy Spirit to those who go on asking him'.

The Gospel finishes with Jesus telling his followers to wait in Jerusalem until they are 'clothed with power from on high'. Luke's interest in the Holy Spirit continues into his second volume, and Acts includes even more frequent references.

3. PRAYER

a) By Jesus

Luke writes about Jesus' prayers far more than any other Gospel author. As noted earlier, the giving of the Spirit at his baptism was in response to prayer from Jesus and this was his first recorded prayer. His last is uttered on the cross: 'Father, into your hands I commit my spirit.'

In between these two, Luke records nine occasions on which Jesus prayed. Seven of these are unique to Luke. Jesus seems to have been **constantly praying to his Father** for direction.

b) By disciples

Luke is also concerned that we should understand the **importance of prayer for every disciple**. Chapter 11 especially includes extensive teaching on this. In addition, the parable of the persistent widow gives encouragement that God is willing to answer prayer, and the parable which follows, contrasting the tax collector and the Pharisee, encourages humility in prayer. Prayer is no less essential for those who would follow Jesus than it was for Jesus himself.

4. JOY

Luke has **more words connected with the root word 'joy' than any other book in the New Testament**. Luke is the only author, for example, to use the word for laughter. He also records the joy in heaven over one sinner who repents. And on one occasion, Jesus was 'full of joy through the Holy Spirit'.

This theme is linked with that of praise and worship. The birth narrative opens with the song of the angels, 'Glory to God in the highest', and finishes in the temple with people 'praising God'. Luke continually **lifts his readers up to heaven**. Some of the most beautiful songs of praise are in

Luke, such as the 'Magnificat' (Mary's song) and the 'Nunc Dimittis' (Simeon's song).

5. THE UNIVERSAL GOSPEL

Luke is the universal Gospel, showing Jesus to be the **Saviour of the whole world**. It is a theme which can be seen throughout the book, as this Gentile writer impresses on his largely Gentile readers how this good news can be for them.

■ He does this first with the genealogy of Jesus. He does not stress his Jewish roots as Matthew does, but goes back to Adam, highlighting the humanity of Jesus and the fact that the gospel is for all: God has always been concerned with *all* peoples.

■ From the very beginning the angels' song includes the words 'peace on earth, good will towards men'.

■ Luke quotes Isaiah, telling us that 'all flesh will see God's salvation'.

■ The Seventy are sent out not to the 'lost sheep of Israel', as the Twelve are directed in Matthew, but to 'every city and place'.

■ We read that 'people will come from east and west and north and south, and will take their places at the feast in the kingdom of God'.

■ At the end of the Gospel Jesus predicts that 'repentance and forgiveness of sins will be preached in his name to all nations'.

So here, faithfully recorded by Luke, is a faith with strong Jewish roots, based in a Jewish context, and which reaches its climax in Jerusalem – all in readiness for the story of Acts, when the faith spreads across the empire, even reaching Rome itself. As such, it is the least Jewish of all the Gospels, as we might expect given Luke's concern to convince the Gentiles of the certainty of the events he records.

How are we to read Luke's Gospel?

A human Gospel

This is a Gospel **for humans lost in sin**. Jesus is the Saviour. Alone of all the Gospels 'salvation' is used as a noun in Luke. Luke wants his readers to know the salvation of Christ, based on the historical events he has described. The verb 'to save' is used more here than in any other New Testament book.

Luke tells us that 'today' is a day of salvation (this is said 11 times, compared to 8 in Matthew and once in Mark), and 'now' salvation has come (14 times, compared to 4 in Matthew and 3 in Mark). He underlines that mercy, forgiveness and reconciliation are available here and now. This salvation comes through the cross of Christ – it is like another baptism for Jesus. Just as the Jewish people were liberated from captivity in Egypt, so his cross provides a new 'exodus' for his people. This, therefore, is a saving Gospel. Luke wants his readers to find salvation in Jesus.

A happy Gospel

The themes of **praise and rejoicing keep recurring**. It is the Gospel that mentions laughter and it has more words connected with joy than any other. In the popular parables in Chapter 15 we see the joy of those who find what was lost, depicting the joy in heaven over the sinner who repents. The response of the disciples to the risen Lord is joy, and the Gospel concludes with rejoicing. In this sense it is attractive and 'user-friendly', an ideal Gospel for the outsider who wants to learn more about Jesus.

A heavenly Gospel

Luke keeps the **focus on heaven**. He stresses the supernatural birth of Jesus, the involvement of the Holy Spirit, and the importance of prayer. He wants those who read it, whatever their background, to be in heaven. The words of Jesus in the parable of the great banquet sum up his concern: 'Go out to the roads and country lanes and make them come in, so that my house will be full.' Luke knows that God has people from all nations he intends to bring into heaven – for Jesus truly is the Saviour of the world.

A most readable Gospel

Luke was able to put the elements of his story together with great skill. We often name the story in Luke 15 the 'parable of the prodigal son', for example. But this is because we fail to see Luke's **abilities as a writer**, and we also fail to appreciate the parable in its context within the Gospel. It is actually the parable of the prodigal *father*, who wasted his money by giving it to his two boys. When you read Chapters 15 and 16 straight through, you can see how the themes flow – and how Luke has carefully composed a most readable Gospel.

Chapter 15 begins with tax collectors and sinners, eating inside a house with Jesus, while Pharisees and scribes murmur outside. The next two chapters all flow out of this setting and explain it. Jesus tells the story of a sheep which is lost; it is far away from where it should be and knows it. Then he speaks of a coin that is lost at home, but does not know it – one story for the men, one for the women, but two 'lost' items.

Then we come to the major story of two lost sons, with the emphasis not on the younger, but the older son. He is more 'lost' than the younger one, but he does not know it. The younger son is therefore like the lost sheep, lost far away and knowing it. The older son is like the lost coin, lost at home but not knowing it.

The parallels do not end there, however, for when we move on to Chapter 16, we again see two characters, corresponding to the two sons in Chapter 15. The first is a puzzling story about a rogue whom Jesus commends for dishonesty. Interestingly, exactly the same word is used to describe the younger son *wasting* his substance in the far country, and for the rogue *wasting* his master's substance. So we have the same word and the same character. Likewise, just as the elder son claimed he did everything right – 'I never broke a command-ment of yours' – so the rich man in the second story in Chapter 16 is not described as guilty of any sin, vice or crime, yet he finishes up in hell because of his indifference to others, his indulgence of himself and his independence from God.

A **unified theme** flows through these parables, therefore, carefully presented by Luke. Sadly our chapter and verse divisions have served to separate what Luke so skilfully and deliberately brought together. The following paraphrase of the stories Jesus told is designed to re-emphasize Luke's unified theme.

Paraphrased parables

Two men and their money (Luke 15–16)

Some time later the spiritual outcasts, some simply irreligious and others downright immoral, gathered around Jesus to hear what he had to say. But the Pharisees and the legal scholars crit-icized him for associating with them and muttered among themselves, 'This fellow seems to enjoy the company of those who don't even *try* to keep God's laws – he actually has meals with them!' So Jesus defended his action by telling them a story.

'Which of you men,' he began, 'owning a flock of 100 sheep and losing one of them, wouldn't leave the 99 in the open field where they were and search everywhere for the lost one until he has found it again? And when he does find it, he's so happy he thinks nothing of carrying it all the way back on his shoulders. When he gets it home, he invites all his friends and neighbours: "Come and celebrate with me – I've found that sheep I'd lost!" I'm telling you, it's exactly the same in heaven; there's more excitement up there over a single sinner who's brought back from his wilful wandering than over 99 respectable citizens who never put a foot wrong!

'Or what woman owning a valuable pendant with 10 silver tokens, and losing one of them, wouldn't get a torch and brush and search every nook and cranny until she has found it again? And when she does find it, she's so happy she invites all her friends and neighbours, "Come and celebrate with me. I just found that coin I'd lost!" I'm telling you, it's exactly the same among God's angels; they also celebrate every time just one sinner has a change of heart.'

Then Jesus added, 'There was once a man with two sons. The younger one went to his father and demanded, "Dad, I want my share of the business now, before you die." So the father divided his assets between the two brothers. Not long afterwards the younger son turned his capital into cash and went abroad. There he squandered his fortune on an extravagant lifestyle. Just when he had spent all his money, that country was hit by a bad harvest which led to a severe shortage of food. Prices rocketed and he soon felt the pinch. To stay alive he hung around a local landowner who let him cart swill to the pigs. Often he longed to stuff his own stomach from the same trough, but no one even thought of giving him anything.

'When he finally came to his senses, he said to himself, "Just think – all those hired hands on my father's farm have more than enough to eat, while here I am, starving to death. I'd better get back to my father again. I'll just say to him,

'I realize I've done a terrible wrong, both against God and against you. I'm not fit to be regarded as your son again, but how about taking me on to the payroll with the other employees?'"

'So he set off home. But while he still had some way to go, his father spotted him coming. He was moved to the depths of his being and ran out to meet his son, threw his arms around his neck and kept kissing him. The son began his prepared speech: "Dad, I realize I've been terribly wrong, from God's viewpoint as well as yours – I just don't deserve to be regarded as your son any more..."

'But his father interrupted him, turned to his servants who had come to see what was happening, and ordered them, "Bring my best suit and get him properly dressed, put my signet ring on his finger and get some shoes for his feet. And slaughter that calf we've been fattening up. We must have a big meal to celebrate such an occasion. My son was as good as dead to me and he's come back into my life again. I thought I'd lost him, but we've found each other again!" So the festivities got under way.

'All this time the elder son had been out working in the fields. As soon as he approached the family home at the end of the day, he heard sounds of a party – people were singing and dancing to a band. So he summoned one of the lads standing around and asked what it was all in aid of. The lad blurted out, "Your brother's back and your father has slaughtered the calf you were fattening because he's home safe and sound."

'The elder brother was furious and refused to go anywhere near. So out rushed the father for the second time that day, to appeal to him to change his attitude. But he exploded in anger, "Look at all the years I've been slaving for you here! Never once have I disobeyed your orders or gone against your wishes. Yet you have never even let me kill a baby goat to have a good time with my pals. But as soon as this son of yours turns up, having swallowed up your hard-earned savings in brothels, then you go and kill the best animal on the farm in his honour!"

'But the father gently replied, "My dear boy, you were the one who stayed here by my side and you know that the remaining estate is already made over to you. Don't you understand that we just had to have this celebration? For here is your brother, who's been as good as dead to us, and now he's living with us again. I thought we'd lost him for ever, but now we've found each other again."'

Jesus went on to tell another story to his own followers. 'Once upon a time there was a wealthy man who employed an agent to manage his estate, and reports reached him that this man was embezzling his capital. So he sent for the man and faced him with it. "What's all this I keep hearing about you? I'm going to have your accounts audited right away. I can't keep you on as manager."

'So the agent considered his future prospects. "What can I possibly do for a living," he said to himself, "now that the boss has given me the sack? I'll make sure that when I'm out of a job there'll be plenty of my former clients who want to help me out."

'So he sent for every tenant who had an outstanding debt to his employer. To the first one who came, he said, "How much do you owe my boss?"

'"Four thousand litres of oil," he replied.

'Then the agent said, "Here is the original contract. Quick, sit down here and alter the figure to two thousand." Later he said to another, "You there. How much did you agree to pay?"

'He replied, "Two hundred sacks of wheat."

'So the agent said, "Here's your agreement; you can cut the figure down by a fifth."

'When the landlord heard about those revised contracts, he couldn't help congratulating the dishonest agent for his quick thinking and shrewd move.

'Sadly it's often the case that those who live for what this world offers show more sense in their business dealings with other people than those who have been enlightened about the other world. So my advice to you is this,' said Jesus. 'Use the world's dirty money to make sure you have plenty of friends, so that when you finally leave all your assets behind, they will welcome you with open arms into heaven itself.

'The man who is trustworthy in trifling matters will have the same integrity in big deals too. And the man who cheats over small amounts will be just as crooked in big business. So if you can't be trusted to handle a corruptible commodity like money, who is going to let you look after anything of lasting value? And if you are unreliable in looking after other people's assets, who will ever think of giving you some of your own?

'No employee can ever work wholeheartedly for two employers. He is bound to make comparisons and will like one better than the other, or be more loyal to one, while being less concerned for the other. That's why you can't devote yourself to making money and serving God at the same time.'

Some Pharisees overheard these remarks of Jesus to his disciples. They managed to be both rich and religious and they sneered at his statement. But he knew what they were thinking and told them, 'You may convince your colleagues, but God sees right through you! Men may be impressed, but God is disgusted.

'The commandments of Moses and the accusations of the prophets were in force right up to the arrival of John the Baptizer. Since then the rule of God has been inaugurated and people are seizing the opportunity to live under it. In fact, it would be easier for planet earth and outer space to disappear than for one iota of divine legislation to be annulled.

'To give you just one example: in God's sight, whoever divorces his wife and marries someone else is living in adultery, and whoever marries a divorced woman also commits adultery.

'There was once a wealthy man, who used to wear the most expensive suits and enjoy lavish meals every day of his life. And there was a poor beggar who sat in the gutter just outside his drive gates, appropriately named God-help-us. His wretched body was a mass of ulcers and he would have given anything just to eat what was thrown into the wastebin up at the house. Stray dogs in the neighbourhood used to lick the matter oozing from his sores. In the course of time, the beggar died and his spirit was escorted by the angels into the loving embrace of Abraham. Shortly after that, the wealthy man passed away and a very impressive funeral took place. But he himself did not attend it. He was already suffering in hell.

'In his agony, he glanced up and spotted Abraham in the far distance, and he was hugging that old beggar, God-help-us! "Father Abraham," he shouted, "have pity on me. I'd even suck that beggar's finger if he'd dip it in some water first! This heat is unbearable!"

'But Abraham solemnly replied, "Just recall how comfortable your life was and how miserable was the lot of my friend God-help-us. Now it is time for him to have a bit of comfort and for you to know what it is to suffer. In any case, there's a huge canyon between us. No one can cross from here to there and no one can get from there to here."

'So the poor rich man thought of another possibility. "I plead with you, then, Father Abraham. If you can't send anyone over here, please send someone to my home on earth. At least my five brothers could be warned about this dreadful place."

'But Abraham shook his head and pointed out, "They have a Bible in the house. If they just read what Moses and the prophets had to say, they'll have all the warning they need."

'But the condemned man disagreed. "That's not enough to convince them, Father Abraham. But if someone came back from the grave to tell them what really happens, they'd surely change their ways."

'But Abraham simply said, "If they won't pay attention to the words God gave through Moses and the other prophets, they are hardly likely to believe someone who tells them he's returned from among the dead."'

PART IV

ACTS

Introduction

When we study any book of the Bible we need to engage with it at two levels. First, we examine the **human level**, considering who was writing and why, aware that each book is rooted in a particular situation with a particular audience in mind. At this level we look at the historical situation, seeking to make the Word of God *real* in its original context.

Second, we consider the book at the **divine level**, asking why the Holy Spirit included the book for us and seeking to determine the way in which it is *relevant* to us today.

We might term these two levels the **historical** and the **existential**. The historical level asks why was it written, what was the human reason behind it? The existential level asks why is it in our Bible and why does God want us to know about this? This two-fold approach will prove especially helpful as we look at the book of Acts.

Acts on a historical level

Who wrote it and why?

THE AUTHOR

The author was Luke, a doctor by profession from Antioch, Syria, and the only Gentile writer in the Bible. He was a companion of Paul, often travelling with him, and had a keen interest in researching the events surrounding the life of Jesus and the growth of the Church. It was probably in Caesarea and Rome that he wrote Luke and Acts respectively (see pages 59–63 for more details on Luke as the author of these two books).

DEFENCE BRIEF

We have seen already that Acts is the second volume of a two-volume work written by Luke, to prepare Paul's defence as he awaited trial in Rome (see pages 63–7). Acts commences by addressing the same man who is referred to at the beginning of Luke's Gospel as the 'most excellent' Theophilus, a title suggesting a lawyer or judge and used elsewhere in Acts of Felix and Festus, both governors who met with Paul. Luke was doubtless aware that his 'brief' might be more widely circulated as people in Rome asked questions about the faith for which Paul stood trial.

Had this been a history of Paul's life, then at the very least Luke would have included the outcome of his trial, if not details of how he died. If this was a history of the Church we would have expected far more details about the church in Rome. But it was not Luke's intention to provide full biographical details about Paul, nor to cover Church history for its own sake, but to give enough information for Theophilus to understand how the Christian faith had developed and why the apostle Paul was now unjustly accused. Hence the readers of Acts are left at the end with the situation which prevailed when Luke had completed the brief for Theophilus.

Structure and outline

Having understood why it was written, the next question concerns the outline of the book, since this also sheds further light on its purpose. There are three commonly held theories concerning Luke's intended structure for Acts.

1. TWO SECTIONS

The simplest theory is that Luke structured Acts around the **two main apostles**. Peter is the apostle to the Jews and dominates Chapters 1–12, and Paul is the apostle to the Gentiles and dominates the rest of the book. There is much to support this theory, since there is a remarkable parallel between what Luke says about Peter and what he says about Paul. It may be that this was intended to counter the threat of two separate churches developing, a Jewish church and a Gentile church, with each claiming their apostle as the one to follow. Luke's account emphasizes that the lives of Paul and Peter were comparable in many respects, so that we should not see one as more important than the other. Here are some of the similarities:

■ They both performed miracles.
■ They both saw visions.
■ They both suffered for their faith.
■ They both made long speeches.
■ They were both filled with the Spirit.
■ They both preached with boldness.
■ They both preached to Gentiles and Jews, though Peter primarily preached to Jews and Paul primarily to Gentiles.
■ They were both imprisoned and miraculously set free.

- They both healed the sick.
- They both healed a congenital cripple.
- They both exorcised demons.
- They both had extraordinary means of healing, Peter with his shadow and Paul with his handkerchief.
- They both raised the dead.
- They both declared judgement on false teachers.
- They both refused worship.
- They both died in Rome (though Luke does not include this in his account).

This analysis strongly suggests that amongst Luke's reasons for writing is this concern to ensure that both men were equally honoured and valued as apostles in the Church. One way of approaching the book of Acts, therefore, is simply to divide it into two sections.

2. THREE SECTIONS

In Acts 1:8 we read, 'You shall be my witnesses beginning in Jerusalem, Judaea and Samaria and to the uttermost parts of the earth.' Some see this statement as the structure Luke follows in developing his themes. The witness for Christ **starts in Jerusalem**, in Chapters 1–7. Chapters 8 to 10 take the witness further **into Judaea and Samaria**, and then finally it spreads from there **to Europe and the heart of the Roman empire**. Thus Luke is seen to be demonstrating how Jesus' words at the beginning had been fulfilled by the end of the book, as the gospel reaches Rome with Paul, the witness of Christ to the Emperor himself. But Rome is hardly 'the ends of the earth'!

3. SIX SECTIONS

The three-stage structure may be compelling in some ways, but there is a better and more detailed way of understanding

Luke's approach. This understanding comes directly from noticing a **literary device** which Luke seems to be using to underline his theme. He includes a **series of similar phrases** at various points in his narrative. Note the following:

■ **Acts 6:7.** 'So the *word of God spread*, the number of disciples in Jerusalem increased rapidly and a large number of priests became obedient to the faith.'

■ **Acts 9:31.** 'Then the *church* throughout Judaea, Galilee and Samaria enjoyed a time of peace. It was strengthened and encouraged by the Holy Spirit, it *grew in numbers*, living in the fear of the Lord.'

■ **Acts 12:24.** 'But the *word of God* continued to increase and *spread*.'

■ **Acts 16:5.** 'So the *churches* were strengthened in the faith and *grew daily in numbers*.'

■ **Acts 19:20.** 'In this way the *word of the Lord spread* widely and grew in power.'

These five statements in Acts about growth in either the Word of God or the Church provide a summary which marks the end of a section. Luke tells us what happened and then he summarizes that because of what happened the Church grew and spread.

In the light of these divisions, the suggestion given above that Luke organizes geographically is partly correct, as these marker verses suggest the following six sections:

1–6:7	Jews in Jerusalem
6:8–9:31	Hellenists and Samaritans
9:32–12:24	Gentiles and Antioch
12:25–16:5	Asia Minor
16:6–19:20	Europe
19:21–28:31	Rome

Luke is describing the 'irresistible force' of this new religion throughout the Roman empire. It is as if the death and resurrection of Jesus are like a stone thrown into a pond. Luke shows how the ripples have spread, with each summary statement underlining that the ripples are continuing, until eventually they reach Rome itself. It is clearly a selective description – the expansion is only depicted in one direction, north-west. The only hint of expansion to the south is the conversion of the Ethiopian on his way home to Africa.

Significant events

Let us now consider some of the events which Luke regarded as significant within this expansion, as he shows the way in which the Christian faith spread from being a rural Jewish movement to an international and cosmopolitan faith.

THE DAY OF PENTECOST

Luke begins with the **first great event in the spreading of the gospel**: the Day of Pentecost (Chapter 2). The Holy Spirit came on 120 disciples in the temple as they gathered for morning prayers at 9 o'clock in Solomon's porch. The gift of tongues accompanying the outpouring was the reversal of God's judgement at the Tower of Babel (in Genesis 11) and enabled the various nationalities gathered at the feast to hear Peter's sermon. Some 3,000 people responded in repentance and baptism and were added to the Church. Many would later return to their home countries to spread the message, including in Rome itself.

THE COMPLAINT OF THE WIDOWS

Surprisingly, Luke records at the beginning of Chapter 6 how the Gentile widows' complaints about not getting a fair share of the food was a key event in the spread of the Church, for it comes directly before the first summary statement in 6:7. The apostles were keen to ensure that there was **no distinction made between the Jews and non-Jews** when it came to aid. A Jewish/Gentile split at this stage was to be avoided at all costs. As a result the apostles selected seven deacons to assist with food distribution. Two of these men, Philip and Stephen, were to make their own impact.

STEPHEN'S MARTYRDOM

Stephen was preaching when he was seized and brought before the religious rulers, accused of spreading anti-Jewish propaganda. We know very little about him from Acts, yet his final sermon is included as one of the longest chapters in the whole book (Chapter 7). His words underline Luke's purpose of describing how Christianity changed from being a Jewish, national religion to being a **Gentile, international faith**.

To the horror of his accusers, Stephen outlines before the Jewish leaders how much of God's activity took place outside their land, before there was a temple. The covenant with Abraham, the rescue from Egypt and the giving of the law were all outside the Promised Land. Their accusations that he was speaking against this holy place and the law were false, therefore, for God's Word and presence transcend national boundaries.

This speech is a theological explanation and justification for the spread of the message to the Gentiles, and within the unfolding drama of Acts it shows how the death of Stephen and subsequent persecution thrust believers out from Jerusalem into Samaria and up as far as Antioch, Luke's birthplace.

PHILIP IN SAMARIA

Luke then records how Philip, another of those seven deacons, went to Samaria and saw many respond to his preaching.

There was a great deal of antipathy between Jews and Samaritans and the disciples themselves had not been altogether generous. The last time John was in Samaria with Jesus, he and his brother James asked if they could pray that God would send fire from heaven to burn all the Samaritans up. Now **many Samaritans came to faith**, and later on Peter and John arrived to pray that the Samaritans would be baptized in the Holy Spirit, asking for fire from heaven for a rather different reason!

Philip was then transported to preach to an Ethiopian eunuch on his way home from Jerusalem. It would seem a curious incident to include, were it not for Luke's purpose of showing how the gospel spread. This is how the gospel came to Ethiopia, brought by that eunuch, the **first African convert**.

THE CONVERSION OF SAUL

Saul's conversion is also a pivotal moment in the whole narrative (Chapter 9). Indeed, this testimony is recorded three times, so that Theophilus might know the evidence given to the other adjudicators. Saul was later known as Paul, and we learn how he was **commissioned to serve Christ** and how he was united with the Jerusalem believers so that they could work to an agreed strategy. Once Barnabas and Paul have been sent out from the church at Antioch, the focus of the book moves from Peter to Paul.

PETER IN CAESAREA

The expansion of the gospel faced a significant stumbling block: the **Jewish food laws** forbade Jews to eat with Gentiles. Luke therefore includes an account of how God taught Peter that eating 'non-kosher' food was permissible and sent him to a Gentile home to preach the gospel.

Acts 10 is a pivotal chapter, showing Peter's astonishment that the **Holy Spirit came upon non-Jews** exactly as he had come upon Jews elsewhere. So crucial was this that Peter had to explain what happened to the apostles in Jerusalem in order that they might be apprised of the way in which God was at work.

THE JERUSALEM COUNCIL

Peter's conversation with the Jerusalem believers is a forerunner to the meeting of the Jerusalem Council in Chapter 15. Paul was sharing the way in which his ministry among the Gentiles had caused the Church to grow. But he was conscious of the danger of a rift developing between the Jewish church and this influx of Gentiles into the kingdom. They had, of course, little or no understanding of the Jewish heritage. The subsequent letter sent to the Gentile churches ensured that the **Gentile church could grow freely** with the encouragement of the 'mother' church in Jerusalem.

COHERENT PURPOSE

It is clear that Luke has selected particular events in order to show Theophilus not just **the fact of the Church's expansion** but also **how it took place**. These are not just haphazard stories. They depict how the Christian faith came to spread across the Roman world and how it remained united despite the cultural pressures it faced. Luke does not tell us of many individual conversions, nor what became of the majority of the apostles, but instead picks out particular events which serve his purpose.

Acts on an existential level

Having looked at the human or historical aspects of Acts, we now need to focus on why the divine editor wanted us to have this book. We must not leave our study in the past, but must also seek to hear its message for today. So we move from the historical significance to the existential meaning of the book, asking what it has to say to us about God now.

Links

Acts is a **vital link between the Gospels and the Epistles**. Imagine the New Testament without it. Many things would be very difficult to understand. People and ideas are mentioned in the Epistles without explanation. Some key people and places cannot be understood without this book.

1. PAUL

Most of the letters in the New Testament are written by Paul, but who was Paul? He was not one of the twelve apostles, so he is not mentioned in the Gospels. Without the book of Acts we would know very little about him or his ministry, or how he came to be writing to churches and individuals and why these letters are important.

2. BAPTISM IN WATER

The baptism of believers is another matter with an important link in Acts. **Only in Acts is it described as being in water**. So while Paul frequently refers to baptism in his *letters* – for example, 'Don't you know that when you were baptized you were baptized into his death?' – he never actually links the word 'baptized' with the word 'water'. This has led some scholars to argue that Paul did not teach water baptism and that 'baptism into Christ' means something purely spiritual. But in Acts you find that Paul was himself baptized and had his converts baptized. So we know that when he talks about 'baptism' in his letters he is talking about baptism in *water*.

3. BAPTISM IN THE SPIRIT

The phrase 'baptized in the Holy Spirit' occurs in all four Gospels, but none of them tells you what it actually means, or what happens when somebody is so baptized. If you looked for a meaning in the Epistles you would also be disappointed. Paul uses the phrase in 1 Corinthians – 'For we were all baptized in one Spirit into one body' – but he does not say what that means in practice. It is only the book of Acts which explains **what it really means to be baptized in the Holy Spirit**, for only there is the event actually described.

4. THE LAW OF MOSES

Acts also helps us when we consider our approach to the law of Moses today. How do we know that we Christians are not bound by it? The law of Moses had 613 different requirements, so we need to be clear whether we are free from these laws or not. How do we know whether or not these are still binding? The answer comes as we read about the great argument concerning circumcision which reached a climax in Acts 15, when it was settled once and for all that **Christians are free from the law of Moses**, though still bound by the law of Christ.

5. THE CHURCH

It is surprising to discover that even the word 'church' could be misunderstood, were it not for Luke's record in Acts. In the Gospels only Matthew mentions the word at all, and his two references are not descriptive of what a church should be like. The Epistles are generally addressed to churches and give us hints as to what they were, but it is only in Acts that we learn **what a church actually was**, including how it was planted, how the apostles appointed elders and what the relationship was between the apostles and the churches they founded.

6. CONVERSION

Acts is crucial to us also because we learn so much about **the proper way in which people were born again**. The Gospels record events before the coming of the Holy Spirit and the Epistles are written to people who are already established in their faith. Neither provides an appropriate model of how people come to faith in Jesus in the Church age. So we go to Acts to see how the apostles brought people into the kingdom, and we read of the normal pattern of *repentance, faith, baptism in water* and *baptism in the Spirit*. (For further explanation of this process, see my book *The Normal Christian Birth*, published by Hodder and Stoughton.)

A model for today

Acts is therefore an important source of information and explanation – but it is clearly much more than that too. Many would see it as a model for church life everywhere, and pine for the day when **modern churches will exhibit the same qualities Luke describes**. This seems a reasonable assumption. After all, it is the only Church history we have in Scripture. Presumably the Holy Spirit wanted it included so that we would know what God intends for his people.

1. BAD AS WELL AS GOOD

Valid though this 'model' approach is, problems do arise if we assume that it is always an *adequate* model. Luke's portrayal is far from idealistic and includes the difficulties as well as the blessings. Acts records **arguments, divisions and mistakes as well as extraordinary growth**.

■ Few would want to hold up the story of Ananias and Sapphira and their deception as model behaviour.

- Simon's flagrant desire to profit by receiving the Holy Spirit does not provide a good model for a young convert wanting to make progress.
- Even the apostle Paul has a 'sharp disagreement' with Barnabas. No blame is attached to either party, but the wording used suggests that it was certainly not ideal preparation for a missionary endeavour.
- Luke describes the attitude of Gamaliel to the new movement. He counsels his fellow leaders to wait and see what happens rather than declare their hands for or against the Christians. But Luke's description does not mean such detached objectivity was an appropriate response and this fence-sitter is not mentioned again.
- By contrast Saul of Tarsus, Gamaliel's student, opts for an aggressive stance. Rather than 'wait and see' he prefers to seek to stop the new faith in its tracks and persecutes the Church. His hostility is overturned on the Damascus road, and this leads him to become a great, perhaps the greatest, apostle.

The account of the community of believers in Acts is therefore a mixture of good and bad. There are rivalries, arguments, hypocrisies, immoralities and heresies. We are given examples of how *not* to do things, as well as models to follow.

2. ABNORMAL AS WELL AS NORMAL

When it comes to understanding events in Acts, there is a distinction to be made between the abnormal and the normal. There were certain things that happened in Acts which were abnormal and **should not be expected to happen continually**.

Take Paul's conversion, for example. He hears the voice of Jesus and is blinded by a light. This was a clearly a one-off experience. If we use this as a paradigm or pattern for modern conversions, not many will pass the test. Indeed, Paul himself claimed it was a unique commissioning for him to be an apostle.

Consider also the death of Ananias and Sapphira. Have believers today not done worse things yet not been slain? Or is the replacement of Judas by casting lots a model for today? Clearly not.

Furthermore, if events are to be repeated, one would be hard pressed to decide which precedent to follow in certain cases. The apostle Peter was saved from Herod, but the apostle James was not. Which outcome should we expect to happen today? We must beware of taking one event or one experience of the early Church and making that a norm for the whole Church in any period.

This discussion brings us to a key question: **How do we distinguish between what is abnormal and what is normal?** Has the Church not often assumed that some phenomena are abnormal and not for today, only to be proved wrong? A series of questions will help us in this kind of decision.

a) Is the event only mentioned once?

If an event is only mentioned once and never repeated, it is likely – though not certain – to be abnormal. On the Day of Pentecost, for example, some things happened which were unique. We do not expect to see wind and flames every time someone receives the Spirit. On another occasion we read that the building shook when the believers met for prayer. This would be an inaccurate guide for us today as to whether genuine prayer had taken place. **Some of the early events were necessarily one-offs**. If something is only mentioned once, therefore, it *may* happen again, but it would be wrong to say that it *must* be repeated.

b) Is the event repeated?

In the descriptions of baptism in the Spirit in Acts, however, we can see some similarities. On the Day of Pentecost the wind and flames are clearly unique, but other phenomena are repeated. When those at the house of Cornelius (10:46) and the disciples of John receive the Spirit, they speak in tongues – suggesting that this may be a repeatable phenomenon, even if the wind and flames are not. Indeed, whenever someone is baptized in the Spirit in Acts, there is always something that happens to make it clear to recipients and onlookers alike that the Spirit has come. **A repeated event increases the likelihood that what we are reading is to be normal for the Church today.**

c) Is there independent confirmation elsewhere in Scripture?

If the Gospels or the Epistles give **independent attestation that the happening in question was a normal part of Christian life at that time, it is pretty certain that we can accept it today.** It is not, for example, just Acts 2:33 that speaks of the Spirit being 'poured out'. Joel 2:17 from the Old Testament and Titus 3:5 in the New confirm this as a term of general validity.

The appointment of elders in Acts is another example. Was this a one-off event? No, it was not just a temporary office in Acts: Titus, 1 Timothy and Hebrews all include references to the universal necessity for this sort of leadership.

3. PRESENT AS WELL AS PAST

Once we have asked the three questions given above, we are better placed to distinguish between the one-off events which were merely part of Luke's historical account and those things which God intends us to recognize as what *should* always happen, even if in the average church today it is a long way from what *does* happen.

It is important that we use these questions and that we use Acts as a model, for if we do not we can fall into the error of believing that another period of Church history is the one we want to duplicate. Many denominational groupings effectively take their cue from such a period, be it the Reformation, the age of the Puritans, the Methodists or the early Pentecostals. They forget that **the Bible provides a sufficient model and is the ultimate standard by which to judge all other ages**.

Acts gives us a model of what the early Church members did and what they were.

What they did

Acts tells of their warm fellowship together, the centrality of the apostles' teaching, the importance of the prayers, and their spontaneous evangelism as the Spirit empowered them and sent them out to tell others about Christ. It also tells of their fearless declaration of the gospel when they faced opposition from Jews and Gentiles alike. It is a vibrant book full of the action of God and the growth of the kingdom.

What they were

They were a people filled with the joy of knowing God, even praising him when they were in prison. They were people who feared God. And they were people of hope and courage: Peter and John were willing to disobey the Jewish leaders and refused to stop preaching. Stephen was also prepared to confront them, even though it meant losing his life.

Acts as a missionary manual

Accepting that Acts is a model for us today, how are we to read it? One of the most helpful approaches was provided by a man writing early in the twentieth century, Roland Allen. He wrote three books which have shaped the thinking of many who seek to understand how Acts should be used today. They are entitled *Missionary Methods – St Paul's or Ours?*, *The Spontaneous Expansion of the Church* and *The Ministry of the Spirit*.

His thinking was far ahead of his time, and I owe much to his insights. He argues that **Acts is not just a model for Church behaviour but a missionary manual for Church expansion.** Acts tells us how to fulfil the Great Commission and spread the gospel. From this one book we can identify a seven-fold strategy which we can follow today.

1. SEND APOSTLES

The word 'apostle' literally means 'sent one'. It was the understanding of the early Church that certain individuals were commissioned by God to spread the gospel. There are five kinds of apostle in the New Testament:

1. Jesus the *Chief Apostle* – there is no one else like him.
2. The 12 apostles, *witnesses of the resurrection* – there is no one like them today.
3. Paul, apostle number 13, the 'last of all born out of due time' – no one is like him today, *writing inspired Scripture*.
4. A *pioneer church planter* who builds new churches with new converts – the apostle Paul would be among this kind too, as would Barnabas and others, who were always sent out in a team.
5. *Any Christian sent from A to B to do anything* is an 'apostle', e.g. Epaphroditus, who was sent to be Paul's housekeeper in Rome – in this sense anyone could be an 'apostle'.

It is the fourth and fifth definitions which apply today. The Church of Jesus Christ needs **church planters and those**

willing to be sent out to accomplish particular tasks in God's name.

The initiative and backing should properly come from the local church. It is clear in Acts that it was the Holy Spirit who set apart the people for the work. The sending out did not come from a decision made by the people, but by the direction of the Spirit. So it was the Spirit who said that Paul and Barnabas should be set aside for the work he had for them. The Church was prepared to send out its best people in order that Christ would be made known.

It is also noteworthy that the apostles were sent out in teams. There was always a minimum of two travelling together (just as Jesus had sent his disciples out two by two). There is no sanction for the 'lone-ranger' missionary in Acts.

2. REACH CITIES

It was common for the apostles to commence work in highly populated centres, so that growing churches could have a ripple effect throughout the surrounding area. So, for example, when Paul went to Ephesus and taught daily in the lecture hall of Tyrannus, we read that 'all the Jews and Greeks who lived in the province of Asia heard the Word of the Lord'. It is likely that a man named Epaphras came to faith through these lectures and planted the church at Colossae. Paul wrote to the church, although he had never visited it himself or been involved in its growth.

It was therefore a sensible and effective strategy to go to the **major urban areas as a bridgehead for further expansion,** and this is something which we need to bear in mind today.

3. PREACH THE GOSPEL

Paul would typically focus first on the synagogue. 'As his custom was, Paul went into the synagogue and on three Sabbath days he reasoned with them from the Scriptures.'

When Paul was with the Jews he would use the Old Testament. But note, too, how **his approach changed according to the audience**. When Paul preached to Jews he quoted the Bible, but when he preached to Gentiles he sought to establish some common ground before introducing biblical concepts. Take, for example, the account in Acts 17 of his address to the Athenians. This was not an especially successful message, though there were some notable converts. Luke includes it so that we might see how Paul addressed a pagan audience.

In his message to the Athenians Paul refers to incidents which took place in their past and to poets whom they knew. He knew that there had been an earthquake in Athens many years before which devastated the city and destroyed their buildings. Being polytheistic, the Athenians assumed that they had upset one of their gods, and were anxious to know which one. So they decided to let some sheep loose in the main street. Whichever idol the sheep lay down nearest to would indicate which god the Athenians had upset. However, the sheep refused to follow the plan and ended up lying down in the middle of a field. So the council met and concluded that if they still did not know which god they had upset there might be a god they had forgotten, who was upset at the absence of an altar for him. So they erected an extra altar, inscribing upon it the words 'To the unknown god'.

Paul, viewing this altar on his visit to the city, uses it as a base from which to tell them of the God they did not know. Immediately he has an audience. From that common ground he can go on to tell them about a God they should and could know, and about Jesus, whom this God raised from the dead and appointed a judge of the human race.

This concentration on preaching the gospel is seen on almost every page of Acts as the Holy Spirit gives the Christians boldness and power to declare their message.

4. MAKE DISCIPLES

The apostles were concerned that people should become 'disciples'. They were not interested in our modern methods of responding: raising a hand, coming to the front of a public meeting or signing a card. They realized that **disciple-making took time** and so Paul would stay in a place for a considerable time to make sure that the believers were established. In Ephesus he taught about the kingdom of God every afternoon from 12 until 4 o'clock (the siesta time) for two years in order that young converts might learn and new people come to faith. Hence, while Luke records how the word 'Christian' was originally coined at Antioch, those who came to faith were more commonly known as 'disciples', or followers of 'the way'. It was **perseverance on the journey** that mattered, not a one-off decision that had little effect on daily life.

5. PLANT CHURCHES

Acts records how the preaching of the gospel established groups of believers and how the apostles revisited these groups later on, so that each missionary journey bore fruit in the **establishment of ongoing communities of believers**. This aspect of the missionary strategy can be easily overlooked if we live in a country where there are already many churches. We fail to see that some churches cater for just one sector of society, perhaps of a relatively narrow sociological type. There are often no existing churches which can reach other groups. This style of church planting ensures that existing churches need not feel that the newcomers are encroaching on their territory, since they will be **reaching an entirely different sociological group**, even if they are geographically very close.

6. APPOINT ELDERS

We read how Paul and Barnabas returned to Lystra, Iconium and Antioch and 'appointed elders for them in each church, and with prayer and fasting, committed them to the Lord, in whom they had put their trust'.

The newness of the churches meant that the 'elders' could only have been 12 months old in the faith, but this was no problem. As long as the candidates were ahead of the others and maturing, they could be **trusted to lead**. This pattern of appointing elders to lead the flock is seen throughout Acts, as the apostles sought to find local leadership so that the communities could become self-governing and not dependent on their founder. It would seem that the elders were appointed by the whole church, with local believers confirming apostolic nominations. (The word for 'appointed' is literally 'hand-raised', so the elders were voted in by a raising of hands.)

In some ways, therefore, the work of an apostle was clearly defined:

- Reaching key cities
- Preaching the gospel whilst adapting it to the hearers
- Making disciples rather than decisions
- Staying with them and training them
- Planting churches so that they left a community behind
- Appointing elders to lead that community

7. APOSTLES LEAVE

This seventh and final stage in the missionary model is also crucial. Once the church was established, the apostle moved on. Further contact may have happened through a letter, a visit, or the sending of an apostolic 'delegate'. **Once a fellowship had local leaders, the apostle could leave them to continue the work**. The churches were self-propagating, self-governing and self-supporting. As such, the ministry of true apostles was mobile. Typically they would also support themselves through a trade and thus not be a financial burden to anyone while the church was being established.

OMISSIONS IN THE PLAN

This analysis of the 'missionary' methods used in Acts has some notable omissions which are often considered essential today.

- There were no church buildings – the believers met in homes or hired buildings.
- Investment in property was not considered necessary.
- There were no clergy–laity distinctions.
- All offices in the church were based on gift and function – and every believer was considered to have a ministry.
- There was no hierarchy.
- There were no headquarters.
- There was no infant baptism.
- There were no churches based on national or denominational lines.
- There were no orders of worship – while we have hints as to how the churches worshipped, we have no set patterns to follow from that time.
- The apostles did not set up hospitals, schools, clinics or aid organizations.

So much of what we regard as a normal part of Church or Christian activity today was not normal for the early Church.

The theological angle

Our consideration of Acts has focused on many areas. We have noted the purpose of the book, the identity of the recipient, the way in which Luke structured his book to achieve his purpose, and how the book can be used as a 'missionary manual'. There is one final way of looking at the book which dovetails with the analysis we have already made, and that is to look at the book from a theological angle. How are we to view it on this level?

Whose acts?

Let us begin with the title. The book was originally called simply 'Acts'. It comes from the Greek word *praxis*, from which we get the word 'practice'. Acts thus describes **the practice of Christianity**, but who is it the practice of? Whose 'acts' are they? There are four possible answers to this.

1. APOSTLES

The book is usually called 'the Acts of the Apostles' which, as we have seen, is quite misleading since **most of the apostles do not appear in it!** James is beheaded in the early chapters, John is mentioned alongside Peter, but only Peter receives much space and more than half the book focuses on Paul, who was not one of the original Twelve. So it is not strictly about the 'Acts of the Apostles'.

2. JESUS

The book begins by saying, 'The former treatise, Theophilus, was about all that Jesus *began* to do and to teach,' thus clearly implying that the present volume is about **all that Jesus *continued* doing and teaching**. Therefore we could call it the 'Acts of Jesus continued'. The name of Jesus is mentioned 40 times in the first 13 chapters. He was the subject of the apostles' preaching and it was in his name that healing was done. So a case can be made for the 'Acts of Jesus'.

3. THE HOLY SPIRIT

Closer study reveals, however, that **the most prominent person in Acts is the Holy Spirit**, who is also mentioned 40 times in the first 13 chapters, and 70 times in all. So perhaps we should call it the 'Acts of the Holy Spirit'. Certainly this would do justice to his role. It is the Holy Spirit who empowers the 120 disciples for witness on the Day of Pentecost and is often described as filling the believers. Some of the big decisions in Acts are due to the direction of the Holy Spirit, and Peter's message at the home of Cornelius is interrupted by the Spirit falling on those present. It was the Spirit who prevented the believers from entering Asia and Bythinia, sending them instead to Troas. He provides the dynamic for the missionary expansion. So it would certainly be valid if we understood the book as the 'Acts of the Holy Spirit'.

4. GOD

This would make sense but for a more important person who is also mentioned prominently in the book. While the Holy Spirit is mentioned 40 times in the first 13 chapters, someone else is mentioned 100 times: God himself. If we make Jesus or the Holy Spirit the focus, this could make us unwittingly 'unitarian' in theology, a trap into which some groups have fallen. **The Holy Spirit focuses us on Jesus, and Jesus brings us back to God.**

The Trinity

So Acts is really Trinitarian in its theology. The word 'Trinity' is not actually in the Bible, but is a short-hand expression for the three persons who make up our one God. Acts is about three things, therefore:

1. The kingdom of God the Father
2. The name of Jesus the Son
3. The power of the Holy Spirit

Thus the best comprehensive title for the book would be the 'Acts of God through Jesus Christ by the Holy Spirit in the Apostles'.

Conclusion

Acts is the remarkable account of the spread of Christianity from Jerusalem to Rome. Luke sifts the evidence and selects the events which chart this expansion, providing a model for church life and a missionary manual to enable the expansion to continue. Simultaneously he achieves his overall goal of briefing Theophilus so that his friend the apostle Paul might be declared innocent at his trial. At the same time God intended that we should understand how he is at work in building his kingdom, so that whoever we are and wherever we live we might be clear about the ideals for which we should work and pray.

PART V

JOHN

Introduction

In the introduction to the Gospels (pages 1–11) we saw that there are three identifiable phases of interest in a great man who has left this world: an interest in what he **did**, in what he **said** and in **what or who he was**. It is clear that John's interest is primarily in this third area. He is looking at Jesus from the *inside* and asking: Who was he?

Matthew, Mark and Luke focus more on what Jesus did and said, rarely tackling questions concerning his inner motivation. It is John who gives us a portrait of **Jesus' inner life and self-identity**. We will see later that this is not his sole reason for writing, but it is an important aspect to grasp if we are to understand the Gospel.

In all there are five major differences from Matthew, Mark and Luke.

1. Omissions

The way John differs from the synoptic Gospels is especially evident when we consider the **content of his Gospel**. It is not just that John writes with a special viewpoint on Jesus, but he omits a number of areas considered significant by the other Gospel writers:

- the conception and birth of Jesus
- his baptism
- his temptations
- the casting out of demons
- the transfiguration
- the Last Supper
- Jesus' struggle in prayer in Gethsemane
- the ascension

These are surprising omissions, especially if we note the prominence which the other writers give to some of these events. The transfiguration, for example, is seen as a pivotal event in the synoptic Gospels. And John was asked by Jesus at the cross to look after his mother, so perhaps he omitted the birth story to save Mary from more publicity. The main reason for these omissions, however, is simply that **such details did not suit John's purpose**. He set out to tell us something quite different from the other Gospels and there was no point in including what he regarded as unnecessary material.

Not only are there omissions, but there is also an **underplaying of some themes** regarded as important or worthy of more space in the other three Gospels. Miracles proliferate in the Gospels of Matthew, Mark and Luke, for example, but in John there are just seven. John also makes little mention of one of the major themes of the preaching of Jesus: the kingdom of God. The word only occurs twice, when Jesus tells Nicodemus that unless he is born again he cannot see the kingdom of God, and when he tells Pilate that his kingdom is not of this world. Again, this does not mean that miracles or the kingdom are unimportant, but just that John has a different purpose from the other writers, and a different way of achieving it.

2. Additions

MIRACLES

Just as there are omissions, there are also some very important additions. Of the seven miracles that John mentions, **five are completely new**:

- the water into wine at the wedding at Cana
- the man by the pool at Bethesda
- the healing of the nobleman's son
- healing the man blind from birth
- the raising of Lazarus

Only two, walking on water and feeding the 5,000, are repetitions.

Furthermore, John uses a **different word for miracles**, referring to them as 'signs'. A sign always points to something beyond itself. So he does not record fewer miracles because he believes them to be less important, but in order to highlight the way in which the miracle or sign points to Jesus. We will note the full impact of this for John's purpose later.

INDIVIDUALS

John includes more stories about individuals and a number of these are unique to his Gospel. Peter's initial refusal to have his feet washed, the conversation with the Samaritan woman at the well, and the conversation with Nicodemus are all included. Indeed, these **one-to-one dialogues** are given more prominence than the meetings with crowds which seem to dominate the other three Gospels. The words of John the Baptist in this Gospel are all in private conversations, not public proclamations.

STATEMENTS ABOUT JESUS

There are also seven big statements about Jesus himself which appear in John, known as the **'I am' sayings**:

- I am the living bread
- I am the light of the world
- I am the door
- I am the good shepherd
- I am the resurrection and the life
- I am the way, the truth and the life
- I am the true vine

These statements only occur in John's Gospel and they serve to emphasize his purpose as he gives us an insight into how Jesus viewed himself.

3. Emphases

The synoptic Gospels are based on the outline of Mark and tend to use his framework of 30 months in the north in Galilee, followed by six months in the south in Judaea, focusing especially on Jerusalem. But John is quite different. Almost all of his Gospel is **in the south** and includes material from Jesus' early ministry. He chooses to emphasize the occasions when Jesus went to Jerusalem for the **feasts** (maybe as often as three times a year). Much of John therefore surrounds the Feast of Tabernacles, the Passover and the dedication of the temple, and ignores much of Jesus' ministry in the north.

4. Style

The style differences in John can be seen especially in two areas.

LANGUAGE

The language of John is different from the other Gospels. They have considerable overlaps, with identical wording being used in places. John's language suggests that his work is **completely independent**. For example, when the synoptic Gospels describe the feeding of the 5,000 they have 53 words in common with each other but just 8 in common with John. Even the word for 'fish' is different.

DISPUTES

The synoptic Gospels major on the parables of Jesus. Longer teaching sections are rare. In John, however, Jesus seems to be involved in **endless arguments**, with **long discourses focusing more on issues of belief than behaviour**. Since these are largely from his southern tours, it does seem that when Jesus went south he changed his style of teaching, probably because he was involved in more arguments with the Judaeans about his identity.

Take the long discussion in John 8, for example. Jesus has been speaking of his relationship to his Father, God. The Pharisees ask Jesus, 'Where is your father?' – the inference being that Jesus could not speak confidently about his parentage and was rumoured to be illegitimate.

'You do not know me or my Father,' Jesus replies. 'If you knew me, you would know my Father also.' So Jesus tells them that he does know who his father is, and turns the argument back on the Pharisees. They should know him too, but are far from him.

This raises an interesting issue concerning Jesus' opponents, which is often not understood. When we read in John's Gospel that the 'Jews' hated Jesus, that Jesus was always arguing with the Jews and that the Jews crucified him, we make a very big mistake if we apply the name 'Jews' to the whole nation. Indeed, this misunderstanding has stimulated anti-Semitism for 2,000 years. When John refers to 'the Jews' he means the southerners, the Judaeans, as distinct from the Galileans in the north, whose attitude (with a few exceptions) was altogether different and more positive towards Jesus.

5. Outlook

John's outlook is very different from that of the synoptics. John was conscious of **the need to communicate to a Greek world as well as a Hebrew one**. He was writing his Gospel in Ephesus in Asia (western Turkey today), where there was a meeting of Greek and Hebrew thought. An understanding of the difference between them is necessary if we are to grasp some of the approaches John uses in arranging his material.

Put simply, the Hebrews used a *horizontal time line* in their thinking, holding the common ideas of past, present and future. They knew God as the One who was, who is and who is to come. All their thinking was on such a time line, where time has both purpose and progress. The Greek mind, by contrast, thought of a *vertical line in space* and was concerned with life above and below, in heaven and on earth.

If you think in Hebrew terms, therefore, you have a concept of time travelling in one direction, with God deciding where things are heading. The first three Gospels assume this sort of time line, and John does not abandon it entirely. After all, he is Jewish himself. He includes, for example, the concept of the 'hour' five times.

However, he also uses the Greek approach, with a vertical line between heaven and earth, above and below. Therefore he sees Jesus as the **one from heaven**, quoting Jesus' words in 3:13: 'No man has ever gone into heaven except the one who came down from heaven – the Son of Man.' And in 6:33: 'For the bread of God is he who comes down from heaven and gives life to the world.'

We saw earlier that there is little mention of the kingdom of God in John's Gospel. Whereas the synoptic Gospels emphasize the kingdom breaking into this present evil age and awaiting the consummation, John focuses more on the *vertical* aspect of God loving the world and sending Jesus down to earth. We could say that John is primarily an 'up and down' Gospel, whereas the others are 'now and then' Gospels.

Understanding John's Gospel

Having considered the ways in which John's Gospel stands apart from the other three, we should take a closer look at John himself.

Who was John?

A FISHERMAN

Before being called to follow Jesus, John was a fisherman involved in both sides of the business, both catching and retailing. We know he had connections in Jerusalem and it is likely that these included a retail business for selling the fish which had been caught in Galilee. So he was **a man of two worlds**, the rural north and the urban city of Jerusalem in the south. As such, he stood out from most of the apostles, who were exclusively northerners – the only native southerner being Judas Iscariot.

A RELATIVE OF JESUS

He was a **cousin** of Jesus and the brother of James, one of the other disciples. Indeed, at least five, and probably seven, of the Twelve were Jesus' relatives, though his own brothers remained sceptical until after the resurrection, when James and Jude not only became believers but penned two of the books of the New Testament. This closeness was evident at the cross, when Jesus asked John to look after his mother.

JESUS' CLOSEST FRIEND

John, however, was not just close to Jesus because he was a cousin. He was also part of an **inner circle**, along with James and Peter, of those who were particularly close to Jesus. He refers to himself as 'the disciple whom Jesus loved', intending to deflect attention from himself by not actually giving his name, but nonetheless providing us with the insight that, of all the Twelve, John was nearest to Jesus. At the Last Supper it was John who was seated next to Jesus as they reclined to eat their meal. Jesus wanted his good friend at hand as they shared this momentous event together.

THE LAST APOSTLE

Not only was John the closest to Jesus, but he was also the last surviving apostle. He writes his Gospel **as an old man**, reflecting on Jesus with unique insight. At the end he records the story of how Peter learned from Jesus that he would be crucified, and how Peter asked Jesus about John's death. Jesus replied that it was none of his business and that if Jesus wanted to keep John alive until he returned, that was up to him. From that day a rumour went round that Jesus would come back before John died, but that is not what Jesus said, and John makes this clear at the end of his Gospel.

The closeness of John to Jesus is reflected in the way in which he **feels free to expand Jesus' actual words**. John paraphrases some of his discourse to bring out the full meaning, because he believes he knows Jesus' mind well enough to explain what he meant. So, for example, if you read John 3:16, 'For God so loved the world that he gave his only begotten Son...', it is not clear who is speaking. Is it Jesus in conversation with Nicodemus, or John expanding the section with reflection of his own? It is certainly a strange thing for Jesus to say, and sounds more like a third person talking about Jesus, in a rather indirect way. This is typical of John throughout the Gospel. He expands what Jesus said because he really understands what he meant. He draws out the implications **under the guidance of the Holy Spirit**. For this reason Eusebius, one of the early Church Fathers, called it 'the spiritual Gospel', and it is easy to see why.

John's purpose

What exactly was John's purpose in writing? Looking at this question will really open up our understanding of the book. Already we have seen John's concern to look at Jesus' inward being, but this was all part of a wider concern which he makes explicit at the end of his Gospel. He tells us that he selected the material **so that readers might believe that Jesus is the Christ, the Son of the living God**, and that by believing this, they might have life in his name. This is a clear enough statement, but it is important that we grasp the *full* meaning of what John says.

EXACT MEANING

We need first of all to understand the precise wording in the original Greek language. Greek has a 'present continuous' tense for verbs which is not easily translated into English, but is so often crucial to a proper understanding of the text. It means to be **continually doing** something. To translate the sense into English it is necessary to add the two little words 'go on'. For example, Jesus did not say, 'Ask and you will receive, seek and you will find, knock and it will be open to you', implying that each action need only be done once. He actually said, '*Go on asking* and you will receive, *go on seeking* and you will find, *go on knocking* and it will be open to you.' So if someone does not receive the Holy Spirit when they first ask, they should not panic: they should go on asking.

This present continuous verb is used by John in 20:31, so that the verse is more properly translated: 'These are written that you may *go on believing* that Jesus was the Son of God and by *going on believing* you will *go on having* life.' This same construction illuminates the best known verse in the Gospel. John 3:16 is better understood as, 'For God so loved the world that he gave his only begotten Son, that whoever *goes on believing* will never perish, but *go on having* eternal life.'

FOR NON-BELIEVERS OR BELIEVERS?

John was not written so that his readers might *start* believing that Jesus is the Son of God. It was written that they might *go on* believing it. Much of the content of John is inappropriate for people who come to the Gospel with no prior knowledge of Jesus. The book is written **for mature Christians**, to help them hold on to their faith so that they do not depart from their understanding of who Jesus is, but go on believing and therefore go on having eternal life.

This was John's principle for the selection of his material. The Gospel was not intended to be comprehensive, but aimed to provide readers with what they needed to know in order that they might continue to have life through constant believing. Put simply, the end for which John was writing was **life** – and the means to that end is **ongoing trust and obedience**.

LIFE IS THE END

John describes the life which Jesus offered as a **present continuous life**. Eternal life includes quantity – it is everlasting; but also quality – it is abundant. It is not just an insurance against death, but a life we are to enjoy here and now. John's

statement of purpose in 20:31 implies that this life is something we possess but may lose if we do not continue to have
faith. So the themes of life and belief are pivotal to John's overall purpose. Life is the end for which he is writing – that his
readers may go on having life – whereas belief is the means to
having this life. If we go on believing, we go on having life.

FAITH IS THE MEANS

That John was concerned with believing is confirmed by the
frequency with which he uses the word – 98 times. This is far
more than the other three Gospels put together. But we need
to be careful, for he does not mean the same thing every time.
For John there are **three stages or phases of belief**.

a) Credence

To give credence means **to believe that something is true**.
The operative word is 'that'. So we believe *that* Jesus died, *that*
he rose again. It is believing in certain historical facts, accepting
the credibility of the gospel, accepting the truth. Credence is
based on the words and works which establish Christ's claims.

This is not by itself saving faith, for at this stage anyone
can say they believe that something is true. It is only the *beginning* of saving faith to accept the truth. (The devil believes the
truth too; he accepts it and he trembles, but he is not a believer.)

b) Confidence

Confidence is the second stage of belief: having accepted the
truth, we then put our confidence *in* Jesus by **trusting and
obeying** him. It means taking the truth and acting on the basis
of what we say is true. Jesus said to Peter towards the end of
the Gospel, 'Follow me' – an activity of confidence, based on
trust and obedience. We may claim to believe in someone, but
if we do not have confidence in them, the trust is superficial.

c) Continuance

This third dimension of belief concerns the ongoing aspect that we considered above when looking at John's main purpose. We are to **go on believing**. In both the Greek and the Hebrew languages 'faith' and 'faithfulness' are the same word, and sometimes we do not know which is meant. If you really trust someone you will go on trusting them. If you are really full of faith then you will be faithful. You will go on believing in someone whatever happens and whatever it costs. Faith, therefore, is not a single *step* (instantaneous) but a *state* (continuous).

Jesus makes this explicit when teaching his disciples in John 15. He uses the imagery of the vine to describe himself and tells them that they are the branches of the vine. He warns them that they must stay, abide, remain in him. If they do not, they will become unfruitful, be cut out and burned. So while John teaches that no one can come to Jesus unless the Father draws him, he also teaches the necessity of the believer *abiding in Christ* if he or she is to enjoy eternal life. Continuance is vital. Faith and faithfulness are both needed.

To summarize what we have noted about John's purpose, therefore: his aim is that readers continue to believe in Jesus so that they will continue to have eternal life. This belief involves the three stages of accepting the truth, acting on the truth and holding on to the truth. Jesus himself is the Truth.

The truth about Jesus

There is a further aspect to John's purpose which will help us understand some of the details of the text. By the time John was writing, around AD 90, there was **considerable speculation concerning Jesus**, even about his early life. A number of 'non-canonical' gospels were written purporting to describe Jesus' childhood. One describes Jesus as a little boy playing in the street in Nazareth. Someone pushed him over into the mud and Jesus cursed him with leprosy. There is also a story of the boy Jesus fashioning little birds out of clay, blessing them and watching them fly away.

Actually Jesus did not do a single miracle until he was 30, because he could not do them without the power of the Holy Spirit. Jesus did miracles not as the Son of God but as the Son of Man, filled with the Spirit. Given the erroneous teaching which was being spread about, John was concerned to silence once and for all speculation concerning Jesus' identity. **Just who was he?** There were in particular two notions circulating in Ephesus which John felt the need to correct.

1. TOO HIGH A VIEW OF JOHN THE BAPTIST

We know from Acts 19 that there was a group in Ephesus who were followers of John the Baptist but had not believed in Jesus until Paul corrected them. In John's day, it seems, there were still those who venerated John the Baptist to the point where there was a danger that they would become a sect of Christianity, **focusing on repentance and morality as John had but without the emphasis on the Holy Spirit which Jesus brought**.

The apostle John set out to write a Gospel that would correct this exalted view of John the Baptist. Every time he mentions John the Baptist he puts him down. He says that John was not the light of the world – he only pointed to the light. He says that John did no miracles. He records John's own words that he must decrease and Jesus increase, that Jesus was the bridegroom while he was just the best man.

John the Baptist said two vital things about Jesus:

■ He will be the **Lamb of God** who takes away the sins of the world.

■ He will be the one who **baptizes in the Holy Spirit**.

Both these things need to be taught if followers are to get a proper balance in their understanding of Jesus. John the Baptist made it clear that *only* Jesus could take away sin and baptize in the Holy Spirit. But in spite of what John had said, his followers had not remembered much of this and Jesus was not given his special place.

2. TOO LOW A VIEW OF JESUS

Much more serious was the fact that in Ephesus they were already holding too low a view of Jesus. This can be understood in part by reflecting on the strong influence of Greek philosophy. As noted earlier, Greek philosophers divided life into two spheres. Various terms are used interchangeably for this: above and below, the physical and the spiritual, the temporal and eternal, the sacred and secular. Not only did they divide these two, they exalted one above the other. Plato said that the spiritual is more real, Aristotle said that the physical is more real.

This being so, the Greeks had a real problem with the teaching that Jesus was both physical and spiritual, earthly and heavenly, human and divine. In their thinking **physical and spiritual could not be put together** like this, and so they developed a number of variations in order to decide which side of reality Jesus was.

1. **More divine than human?** Some said Jesus was more divine than human, that he was never truly human but just *appeared* as a human being. This heresy was known as 'docetism', from a word meaning 'phantom' – i.e. Jesus was only seen as God in a human form. According to this view Jesus never really experienced humanity, for his deity always overshadowed his human side.

2. **More human than divine?** Others said he was more human than divine, a man who responded perfectly to God and developed fully the capacity of the divine that is in all of us. This is termed 'adoptionism' – i.e. Jesus was only *adopted* as God's Son, usually thought to have happened at his baptism when he was filled with the Spirit. Sadly, this is a heresy still being taught today.

3. **Partly human, partly divine?** Some argue that he was partly divine and partly human without saying he was more one than the other. This view is still current today. The Jehovah's Witnesses argue that we must view Jesus as a demi-God, semi-human, the first *created* being. Since the first verse of John explicitly states that he was God, and was with God in the beginning, the Jehovah's Witnesses translate the passage to say that he was *a* God, inserting an indefinite article that is not in the original Greek.

4. **Fully human, fully divine?** John's Gospel clearly asserts that Jesus is both fully divine *and* fully human. It was crucial for this to be demonstrated if John's purpose was to be achieved. Only one who was fully divine and fully human could save mankind from sin – his *humanity* enabling him to die on our behalf and his *divinity* ensuring that he would conquer death and offer life to those who would believe in him. If John's readers were to have life in Jesus' name, they must know the *same* Jesus the apostles knew.

John therefore wanted people to know the truth about Jesus and so he deliberately focused on these two areas, on Jesus' humanity and divinity.

1. HIS REAL HUMANITY

Jesus is actually 'more human' in the fourth Gospel than in the other three. Take, for example, the shortest verse in the Bible:

'Jesus wept.' It shows Jesus as fully human, standing at the grave of one of his best friends, knowing that soon he would be calling him from the grave, yet weeping at the situation. John records Jesus being hungry and thirsty, tired and surprised, all thoroughly human characteristics. Pilate unwittingly sums up what John was portraying with the words, 'Behold, the man!' In Jesus John shows us **what humanity is really like**, or what it should be.

This humanity is also seen in John's emphasis on Jesus' **prayer life**, where more detail is given than in the other Gospels. John depicts a truly human Jesus who needed to pray, depending on his Father to direct what he said and what he did. Some of his most beautiful prayers are in this Gospel.

Furthermore, the Gospel's focus on the **death of Jesus** emphasizes as no other that he really died. John records how one of the soldiers pierced Jesus' side with a spear, bringing a sudden gush of blood and water. Then John adds the sentence, 'He knows that he tells the truth, and he testifies so that you also may believe.' It was important to John that his readers should know that Jesus was really dead. Incidentally, this extraordinary symptom indicates a ruptured pericardium, a 'broken heart'.

By the same token, John also provides eyewitness evidence of the **resurrection**, recording his observation of the strips of linen and the head cloth in the empty tomb. Not only was Jesus really dead, but he was really raised from the dead.

2. HIS DIVINITY

The main emphasis in John, however, is on the **full divinity of Jesus**. This takes us back to John's purpose for his Gospel, and gives us the opportunity to look closely at the intriguing way in which John develops this. We have seen already how John recognizes that faith begins with credence, the belief that something is so. John makes the case for belief that Jesus is fully divine by organizing his evidence around the figure seven, the perfect number in Hebrew thinking. John includes in his Gospel **three complete bodies of evidence for Jesus' divinity**: seven witnesses, seven miracles and seven words.

a) Seven witnesses

The word 'witness' is used 50 times in the fourth Gospel. John stresses that we have **personal testimonies** to the truth about Jesus. There are seven people who attribute divinity to Jesus in this Gospel:

- John the Baptist
- Nathanael
- Peter
- Martha (the first woman to do so)
- Thomas
- John, the beloved apostle
- Jesus himself

In Jewish law two or three witnesses would be enough to establish the truth, but here John includes the perfect number of people to testify that Jesus really is the Son of the living God.

b) Seven miracles

We noted earlier how John records just seven miracles in all, and he calls them 'signs' because they point to who Jesus was. He actually includes the seven miracles (signs) which were the most supernatural and sensational works that Jesus performed. He does not include casting out demons, because there were plenty of people doing that in the ancient world, including the Pharisees. Instead he highlights **miracles no one else could do**:

- Turning water into wine – an unmistakable miracle.
- Healing the nobleman's son while miles away from the sick person, without seeing or laying hands on him.
- Healing the man by the Pool of Bethesda who had been there for 38 years, clearly suffering from a chronic condition.
- Feeding the 5,000, a miracle which all four Gospels include – a creative miracle, producing a lot from a little.
- Walking on water.
- Giving sight to the man blind from birth.
- Raising Lazarus from the dead – not the resuscitation of a corpse soon after death, as with Jairus' daughter or the widow of Nain's son, but the raising of a man whose body would already have started to rot.

John is saying that these are 'signs' pointing to the divinity of Jesus. As Nicodemus said, no man could do the things Jesus was doing unless God was with him.

c) Seven words

John uniquely records for us seven 'words' which Jesus gave about himself, mentioned earlier. To Jewish ears his claim was unmistakable, for each time he began with the Hebrew word for God, YHWH, meaning 'I am'. John carefully includes these sayings **in settings which demonstrate that Jesus' claim was legitimate**.

- 'I am the bread of heaven' was delivered following the feeding of the 5,000 with five loaves and two fish.
- 'I am the light of the world' followed his giving sight to the man born blind.
- 'I am the resurrection and the life' was said as he brought Lazarus out from the grave.

He also said, 'I am the door', 'I am the good shepherd', 'I am the way, the truth and the life', and 'I am the true vine'. This is a man who knew himself to be God in human flesh and these seven words, placed deliberately throughout the Gospel, are crucial to John's case that Jesus is worthy of the readers' trust.

Open relationship to the Father

In John's Gospel, Jesus' relationship to the Father is far more open than in the synoptics. John records that Jesus was **sent** by the Father, **one** with the Father, and **obedient** to the Father in the words he speaks and in the works he does.

So much of Jesus' controversy with the Jews concerned his identity and this was what created the greatest animosity, especially when he claimed to be God: '"I tell you the truth," Jesus answered, "before Abraham was born, I am!" At this they picked up stones to stone him, but Jesus hid himself, slipping away from the temple grounds.'

In fact, John is the only Gospel directly to describe Jesus as God, though the implication is there in the other three. John begins with the statement 'the Word was God' and towards the end Thomas confesses Jesus as 'my Lord and my God'.

Themes

We come finally to consider the themes which are integral to John's overall purpose that faith in Christ might be continued.

1. Glory

'Glory' is a key word in John, for it was a word which the Old Testament reserved for God himself. In the very first chapter, John uses the same word for the Word dwelling among men as is used of the *shekinah* glory of God when he revealed himself through the tabernacle at the end of Exodus. John saw this splendour of God in Jesus throughout his whole life, death, resurrection and ascension. Even the cross was a place where Jesus was glorified. From the very start, therefore, we are introduced to a man who is **utterly distinct** from his contemporaries and set apart from all other men of God.

2. Logos

John starts his Gospel in a unique way. When Mark wrote his account of Jesus, he began when Jesus was 30 years of age, since this was when he first sprang into public view. Matthew was the author of possibly the next Gospel to be written, but decided to go further back, arguing that it was necessary to include Jesus' conception and birth, and because he was a Jew, the genealogy had to go back to Abraham. Luke felt that, since Jesus was the Son of Man, he must be seen as a human being belonging to the whole human race, and so he started his genealogy with Adam.

In contrast to the other three, John decides to begin even earlier, emphasizing that Jesus existed before creation. So he takes the words from Genesis 1:1 as the basis for his opening to the Gospel: 'In the beginning was the Word, and the Word was with God, and the Word was God' (see the paraphrase of John's opening on pages 149–51).

JESUS' NAME

An interesting question arises here which will help us to understand what John wrote. **What do you call Jesus before he was born?** We are so used to speaking of 'Jesus' that we forget this was a brand-new name, given when he came to earth. So what was he before? If John is to write of one who existed at the very beginning, what should he call him?

John chose a unique name: 'the Logos', translated as 'the Word' in most Bible versions. He chose it because it expresses so well who Jesus was, in a way which would make sense to those who were reading. We generally think of 'a word' as an expressed thought that comes out of the mouth and into the ear. A word is expressed by one person and affects another. In this sense Jesus is a **communication** – a word from God to us.

BACKGROUND TO 'LOGOS'

A little history will help explain why John chose to call Jesus the Logos. This concept had particular meaning in Ephesus, where John was writing. Six hundred years before there lived in Ephesus a man called Heraclitus, acknowledged as the founder of science. He believed in the necessity of **scientific enquiry**, probing the natural world, asking how and why things were the way they were. Was it merely chance? Were we in a chaotic universe or was there an order?

He looked for patterns or 'laws' to see if he could deduce some logic behind the operation of the natural world. He used the word *logos* to stand for 'the reason why', **the purpose behind what took place**. When he looked at life (*bios*) he looked for the *logos*; when he studied the weather (*meteor*) he sought the *logos*. This concept now appears in our words for the study of different areas in science: biology, meteorology, geology, psychology, sociology, etc.

So Heraclitus said that the *logos* is 'the reason why'. Every branch of science is looking for the *logos*, the reason why things are as they are. John, realizing that **Jesus is the ultimate reason 'why' everything happened**, took up this idea and called Jesus the *logos*, 'the Word'. The whole universe was made for him. He was the Logos before there was anyone else to communicate with. That is the reason why we are here. It is all going to be summed up in him. He is the 'Reason Why'.

The word has another phase in its history too, this time across the Mediterranean Sea from Ephesus in Alexandria, Egypt. Alexandria had a school which combined Greek and Hebrew thinking, in part because there were many dispersed Jews living in the city. This school, or university, was the location for the translation of the Old Testament into Greek by 70 scholars known as the 'Septuagint' or 'LXX'. One of the Jews involved was a professor called Philo. In seeking to interpret Hebrew thinking into Greek, Professor Philo seized on the word *Logos* and said that the Logos was not to be spoken of as 'it', but as 'he'. He was **'personifying'** the Logos, rather in the way that in Proverbs wisdom is personified as a woman.

THE LIVING WORD

John combines the thinking of Heraclitus and Philo. There is an organizing principle, a 'why' at the root of everything, and this Logos is not just to be personified: he is a person and his name is Jesus. He is the Word, with a capital 'W', the one and only living Word.

On the first page of his Gospel, John says four absolutely vital things about the Logos.

1. **His eternity**. In the beginning the Logos was *already* there. We cannot go further back in our imagination than the beginning of the universe. He was not created, but has equal status with God as creator of the world.

2. **His personality**. 'The Logos was *face to face* with God.' That is the literal translation. It is the word used of two people looking into each other's eyes and loving one another. Christians are the only people on earth who can say that God is love, because they are the only people who believe that God is three in one. The Jews and the Moslems cannot say that he *is* love, because they believe he is just one

person, and love is impossible for just one person. God is more than one person, and if he is father and son loving each other, you can say that he is love and always was love.

3. **His deity**. In the beginning the Logos was already there, face to face with God in a personal relationship, and he '*was God*'. The Logos was not created, nor was he any less than God: he was totally equal to God. When Thomas exclaimed, 'My Lord and my God!' he stated the truth about Jesus. He was there at the beginning involved in creation. Scientists today speak of the earth's crust as being made up of 'tectonic plates'. The word relates to the Greek word *tecton*, which means 'carpenter'! Jesus, the carpenter from Nazareth, made our planet. He is the source of light and life. Everything exists for his pleasure.

4. **His humanity**. A little later in the first chapter we read the amazing words: 'The Logos *became flesh* and pitched his tent amongst us, and we beheld his glory, glory such as you would only see in the begotten Son of the Father.' It is possible to know God personally. Jesus is God with a face. God is Jesus everywhere.

With this staggering first chapter John is declaring from the outset that there are valid reasons for believing.

- Since Jesus is eternal, he can give us everlasting life.
- Because of his personality we can experience a personal relationship with him.
- In his deity he and he alone can forgive sins.
- In his humanity he can make atonement for us.

3. Life

If the Logos theme commences the Gospel, 'life' is an important theme which runs throughout, mentioned 34 times. As we saw earlier, the Gospel is written so that Christians might go on believing and go on having life in Christ. We noted too that this life is *abundant* and *present* as well as *everlasting*. John draws a series of contrasts as to what this life will mean for the believer.

LIFE/DEATH

He explains that having this life means that **believers will not see death**. Life will just continue beyond death. Death cannot touch it. So he contrasts those who are certain to die with those who will never die. 'For my Father's will is that everyone who looks to the Son and believes in him shall have eternal life, and I shall raise him up on the last day.'

LIGHT/DARKNESS

John also uses the contrast of light and darkness. When Jesus speaks of 'never walking in darkness', he is referring to **moral darkness**. He says that if we walk with him we will not have things to hide, for we are walking in the light with everything above board and no secrets. Darkness, however, is the metaphor for death and an absence of God. Jesus says, 'I am the light of the world. Whoever follows me will never walk in darkness, but will have the light of life.'

TRUTH/LIES

We have noted how John highlights the three stages of accepting the truth, doing the truth and holding to the truth, if faith is to be genuine. But he also contrasts truth with lies and includes a whole section in Chapter 8 where this theme dominates a discussion between Jesus and his opponents. The word for 'truth' and the word for 'real' are the same in the Hebrew and Greek languages. **If we live in the truth, we are also living in reality**. Jesus says, 'If you hold to my teaching, you are really my disciples. Then you will know the truth, and the truth will set you free.'

FREEDOM/SLAVERY

This was a discussion point between Jesus and the Pharisees, who claimed never to have been slaves to anyone but had clearly forgotten the slavery in Egypt! Jesus said that whoever sins is a slave to sin, because every time you sin you help to strengthen the chain of habit that will be your master. He had come to set them free. True life, therefore, meant **freedom from spiritual bondage**. 'So if the Son sets you free, you will be free indeed.'

LOVE/WRATH

John is clear in his understanding of two contrasting aspects of God's activity. A person is either in God's love or under his wrath. There is no middle way. The **eternal consequence** of one as opposed to the other is made very clear. Jesus says, 'Whoever believes in the Son has eternal life, but whoever rejects the Son will not see life, for God's wrath remains on him.'

REAL LIFE

Real life, therefore, is a **personal relationship with Jesus and his Father**. It is life in the light and the truth, in freedom and love. Praying to his Father, Jesus says, 'Now this is eternal life: that they may know you, the only true God, and Jesus Christ, whom you have sent.'

4. Holy Spirit

No Gospel tells us as much about the Holy Spirit as John. As such, it is well placed before the book of Acts, in spite of Acts having such strong links with Luke's Gospel. It is through the

Holy Spirit that we can enjoy the life which John describes. The teaching on the Holy Spirit is therefore prominent in John's writing.

■ In Chapter 1 John the Baptist testifies that Jesus received the Holy Spirit and that he will **baptize** others in the Holy Spirit.

■ In Chapter 3 Jesus talks about the necessity of being **born of water and the Spirit**, before we can enter the kingdom.

■ In Chapter 4 Jesus speaks of the Spirit as **living water** and says we must worship God **in Spirit and in truth**.

■ In Chapter 7 Jesus goes to the Feast of Tabernacles in Jerusalem, the feast being held in September or October at the end of the dry season. On the last day of Tabernacles the Jews enacted a ceremony in which the priests filled up a great pitcher with water at the Pool of Siloam, carried it to the temple and poured the water on the altar, while praying for the early autumn rains. On this occasion Jesus stood up and called out, 'If anyone is thirsty, let him come to me. I will give him a **spring of living water**, gushing up in his innermost being.' The text tells us that he was speaking about the Holy Spirit, whom those who already believed in him were later to receive.

■ Chapters 14 to 16 are full of the new '**Comforter**' who is going to come, the Spirit of truth. The Greek name for the Holy Spirit is *paraclete* (*para* meaning 'alongside', *cletus* meaning 'called') – the one who stands by you, or the one who is called alongside. The Holy Spirit is also described as one who is just the same as Jesus. He will continue the work of Jesus after he has left, convicting the world of sin, righteousness and judgement, empowering believers and reminding them of everything Jesus said.

■ In Chapter 20 Jesus prepares his followers for the **Day of Pentecost** by giving them a sign and a command. The sign was Jesus blowing on each of them, and the command was, 'Receive the Holy Spirit.' They did not receive anything at that moment, but it was a rehearsal for Pentecost a few weeks later. That day, when they were seated in the temple, they heard the sound of the wind, reminding them of what Jesus had done. Then they obeyed his command and received the Holy Spirit he had promised.

John's opening paraphrased

John's opening statements are crucial to the purpose in his writing a Gospel. Yet they are so profound that even believers can feel out of their depth – another confirmation that this is not the most helpful Gospel to distribute amongst unbelievers. The following paraphrase is intended to make the passage more 'user-friendly', translating 'Logos' as earlier defined ('the reason why').

> At the very first moment of its existence, the whole reason for our universe was already there and had been there from all eternity. Both the purpose and pattern of it all were to be found in a person, someone who could look God in the face because he too was fully divine. From the start of what we call 'Time', he was working alongside the creator. It was through this partnership that everything else came into being. In fact, not one thing was made without his personal involvement. Even life itself originated in him and his own life sheds light on the meaning of life for every member of the human race. His light goes on shining through all the gloom of human history, because no amount of darkness can ever extinguish it.

In the course of time a man appeared with a special commission from God himself. His name was John and he came to announce the imminent appearance of this light of life, so that everyone could put their faith in God by getting to know this person. John himself could not enlighten anyone, but God sent him to point out the one who would. The real illumination was already entering the world at that very time and was going to show everybody up by shining among them. He came right into this world, the world he himself had brought into being – yet the world did not recognize him for who he was! He arrived at his very own place, but his own people would not give him a welcome. Some did accept him, however, using his name with utter confidence, and these were given his authority to regard themselves as God's new family – which, indeed, they were now by birth, not because of their physical beginnings (whether that was a result of impulsive urges or deliberate choice), but by the direct act of God.

So this divine person, who was the reason behind our whole universe, changed into a human being and pitched his tent among ours. We were spectators of his dazzling brilliance, which could only have radiated from God's very own Son, shot through with generosity and integrity.

John was a reliable witness and shouted to the crowds: 'This is the person I've been telling you about. I told you that my successor would take precedence over me, because he was around before I was even born.'

And we also have benefited so much from all that he had in such full measure, receiving one undeserved

favour after another. All we got through Moses were
strict rules which we had to try to keep, but the help
and the honesty we needed to live right came through
Jesus, the real Messiah. Nobody had ever before had
the chance to see God as he really is; now God's very
own Son, who has been closer to his Father than anyone else, has shown us everything we need to know
about him.

Conclusion

John is a remarkable Gospel, utterly different from the other
three. It reflects the unique insights of the man who was closest
to Jesus while he was on earth, and is full of a concern that we
should not just know about what Jesus did, but should also
realize who he was. It reflects, too, John's burden that believers
in Jesus should not be side-tracked by erroneous teaching,
whether concerning Jesus' identity or the veracity of his
claims. He wanted believers to be absolutely sure that eyewitnesses, Jesus' own words and his astonishing works all point to
one who was truly God come in the flesh, the living Word, the
very glory of God among man. John's collected evidence and
proof all make the most compelling testimony to Jesus' right to
demand our ongoing trust and obedience.